The Pursuit of Meaning

VIKTOR FRANKL, LOGOTHERAPY, AND LIFE

JOSEPH B. FABRY

REVISED EDITION

HARPER & ROW, PUBLISHERS

SAN FRANCISCO

1817

Cambridge
Hagerstown
Philadelphia
New York

London
Mexico City
São Paulo
Sydney

THE PURSUIT OF MEANING: *Viktor Frankl, Logotherapy, and Life,* Revised
Edition. Copyright © 1968, 1980 by Joseph B. Fabry. All rights reserved.
Printed in the United States of America. No part of this book may be used
or reproduced in any manner whatsoever without written permission except in the case of brief quotations embodied in critical articles and re-
views. For information address Harper & Row, Publishers, Inc., 10 East
53rd Street, New York, NY 10022. Published simultaneously in Canada by
Fitzhenry & Whiteside Limited, Toronto.

FIRST EDITION

*the text of this book is printed
on 100% recycled paper*

Designed by Jim Mennick

Library of Congress Cataloging in Publication Data
Fabry, Joseph B.
THE PURSUIT OF MEANING.
Bibliography: p. 175
Includes index.
1. Logotherapy.   2. Frankl, Viktor Emil.
I. Title.
RC489.L6F33   1980   616.8'91   79-2981
ISBN 0-06-250302-2

80 81 82 83 84 10 9 8 7 6 5 4 3 2 1

TO JUDITH,
who taught me the meaning of being a husband;

TO WENDY, CLAIRE, AND RICHARD,
who showed me the meaning of being a father;

AND TO MAX,
who demonstrated the meaning of being a friend.

Contents

Foreword

I truly appreciate that Dr. Fabry has been given the opportunity to thoroughly revise his book on logotherapy, providing new readers with an introduction to this school of thought and readers already familiar with logotherapy with the exposure to the present state of research in this field.

In bringing his book up to date, Dr. Fabry took into account the innovative and creative contributions logotherapists throughout the world have made since his book was first published in 1968. As the executive director of the Institute of Logotherapy in Berkeley, California, and as the editor of *The International Forum for Logotherapy*, he has kept in close touch with other logotherapists and the growing literature on logotherapy, both in English and German, in addition to his continuous contact with me during my American lecture tours (on one of which we first met in 1963) and on his frequent visits in Vienna.

Since 1968, three more of my books have been published in English: *The Will to Meaning: Foundations and Applications of Logotherapy; The Unconscious God: Psychotherapy and Theology;* and *The Unheard Cry for Meaning: Psychotherapy and Humanism*. Dr. Fabry has considered these books, as well as many recent journal articles, in the present version of *The Pursuit of Meaning: Viktor Frankl, Logotherapy, and Life*.

Most remarkable, however, is his attempt to analyze the changes the world at large has undergone in the meantime. He hypothesizes that the rebellions of the sixties have evolved into a more goal-oriented groping toward meanings in the seventies and that logotherapy may well meet this need.

One of Dr. Fabry's most significant contributions is the development of his own version of logotherapeutic group sessions. In them he not only applies logotherapy but extends it and builds on it; and he does it, to his credit, without denying its source. His unique contribution, however, is making logotherapy available to the general public. Thus more than anyone else he was qualified to provide readers with a popular presentation of the teaching body called logotherapy, enabling them to apply it to their lives. Even the professional representatives of the helping professions, be they counselors, ministers, or therapists, may benefit from the cross-fertilization he has brought about. Many Americans have confided to me that some of the logotherapeutic ideas and concepts they first encountered in my writings became completely clear to them only when they read them again in Dr. Fabry's formulations.

In my original preface I wrote that Dr. Fabry set himself a threefold goal: to popularize logotherapy without vulgarizing it; to simplify its theories without oversimplifying them; and to "Americanize" its practice by focusing on those aspects that speak to readers in the cultural climate of present-day America. I know now from reader reactions that he was successful not only in the United States but— through the translations of his book—also in Germany, Austria, Switzerland, Italy, Greece, Japan, and the Spanish-speaking world. By his fresh and anecdotal style and his ability to illustrate my theories with vivid examples, he has been able to help his readers overcome frustration and find direction in situations of emptiness, doubt, and despair.

Ten years ago I expressed the hope that Dr. Fabry would be rewarded by the impact and influence his book will have on the lives of its readers. Today I know my hope has been fulfilled. My wish for the revised version is that what a wise man said of American medicine may come true: that fame comes not only to those who conceive an idea but to those who make the idea popular—who help people understand it.

Viktor E. Frankl

Acknowledgments

I thank Dr. Viktor Frankl, who has become a friend as well as an inspiration, for his continued and extensive help as this book goes into a revised and updated edition and his wife, Eleonore, who typed her husband's voluminous correspondence, which kept our dialogue open over a distance of six thousand miles.

I am also grateful to my wife, Judith, for her human, editorial, and secretarial assistance, and to Hyman Roudman for his editorial suggestions.

Introduction

For the past ten years I have been helping people "apply logotherapy to life" through sharing groups in universities, colleges, growth centers, churches, social service organizations, and in the Institute of Logotherapy. The most striking phenomenon in such groups has been the extent of what is called in logotherapy "the existential vacuum," an inner emptiness especially observable among people in transition periods—the young deciding on a career; those dissatisfied with their work and wishing to change; jobholders approaching retirement; men and women thinking about marriage or divorce; people divorced or widowed; couples, especially women, after their children leave home; and individuals who are sick or facing old age or death. Many felt lonely, empty, frustrated, trapped, and unhappy. The values that guided former generations toward meaning were no longer trusted, and inner sources of meaning had not yet developed. Between rejection of traditional values and inability to find individual meaning an inner emptiness had opened up.

Logotherapy is "therapy through meaning," guiding people toward understanding themselves as they are and *could be* and their place in the totality of living. This self-appraisal is not done by wishful thinking; it is based on the realities of life, acknowledging the existence of injustice, suffering, and the certainty of death. Logotherapy is an existential therapy based on actual experiences. It helps us have a fresh look at ourselves, our limitations and potentials, failures and visions, our total experiences, with people to encounter, disappointments to overcome, hopes to realize, and tasks to fulfill. This perception is based on the intuitive knowledge that life has meaning, however obscure it may seem at times; that every one is motivated by what Frankl calls "the will to meaning," however repressed it may be; and that everyone has the freedom, however limited, to discover meaning. The belief in meaning, the will to find it, and the freedom to search for it are the tenets of logotherapy. Most people need not be persuaded that meaning exists and that they yearn for it; they merely have to be made aware of what, in the depth of their unconscious, they know to be true.

Logotherapy is supportive on still another level, and that is what distinguishes it from most other therapies: It marshals the forces of the human spirit. It draws our attention to the storehouse of specifically human resources within ourselves on which we can rely to restore and maintain our mental health. The human spirit has always been the focal point of religion, but logotherapy shows it to be available to all human beings, whatever their religious, humanistic, or atheistic bent may be.

How to Find Meaning

This book cannot tell readers how to find meaning in their particular situations. Only they can do that. Logotherapy opens doors but we select the doors through which we wish to go on our search. A repressed or ignored will to meaning may cause a feeling of emptiness, but this in itself is no disease. From the vantage point of logotherapy it is rather proof of humanness: only humans search for meanings, have doubts, and feel frustrated about not finding them. To dwell on emptiness and frustration only increases these feelings. To fear that this inner emptiness is a first step to sickness will enhance the possibility that a neurosis may indeed invade the vacuum. The way to overcome the existential vacuum is not by fearful self-observation, not by trying to fill it with "fun," power, money, drugs, or excitement, but by filling it with meaning.

Logotherapy sees meaning on two levels. First, as ultimate meaning, a universal order in which every person has a place. We see order in religious or secular terms, depending on our world view. In addition to the question "Where do I fit into the whole of life?" the search for meaning raises questions as to our identity, purpose, direction, and tasks: "Who am I? What is my purpose? Where am I going? What ought I to do?" The existence of ultimate meaning cannot be proved, except in the unrepeatable experimentation of living. We can live *as if* meaning, order, purpose, direction, and tasks exist, or we can live *as if* everything were arbitrary and see which alternative points to fulfillment. The proof comes not from ever reaching and holding the meaning of life, which is as impossible as reaching and holding the ever-receding horizon. The proof lies in the fulfillment that comes with the search.

On a second level, however, there *are* meanings that we can, indeed must, find to fill our existential vacuum. Just as we cannot find *the* truth but many truthful statements, so we cannot find *the* meaning but many meaningful experiences. Logotherapy offers a daring concept: Each person is a unique individual going through a sequence of unrepeatable moments each offering a specific meaning to be recognized and responded to. In most situations the "meaning of the moment" is nothing spectacular—to get up in the morning, eat breakfast, drive safely, do our work. Some moments, however, are subtler: to help a friend, to listen to another person, to make a commitment. Occasionally, we are challenged by conflicting choices: to enjoy a quiet evening at home or visit a friend; to take our family on a picnic or fix a garden fence. Occasionally, we face moments of vital decisions: to marry, to have a child, to decide on a career, to retire.

But Frankl cautions that we cannot invent meanings arbitrarily; we can only discover the meaning inherent in the situation. Often we must make our decision on the basis of insufficient information, but we cannot wait until all the facts are in. We must rely on our conscious knowledge and unconscious intuition and on the voice of our conscience, feeble and prone to error as it is. Chapter V presents the logotherapeutic concept of the conscience. It enables us, under certain circumstances, to take a stand against traditional solutions, customs, laws, environmental influences, impulses, drives, even physical limitations. As Frankl points out, we may not be able to free ourselves *from* these limitations, but we always have the capacity to take a stand *toward* them.

The search for meaning is a never-ending attempt to make sense of life in spite of apparent chaos and arbitrariness. We cannot find meaning once and for all, just step by step. The search requires patience and flexibility—patience because the meaning of a situation sometimes is revealed only later, flexibility because what is meaningful in one situation must not become frozen into a pattern that loses its validity as life goes on. It is preferable to pursue meaning from both ends, to have long-range goals and to approach them step by step. This approach is not always possible (when we can see no long-range goals and have to rely on our immediate responses to the calls of the moment, in hope that goals will eventually emerge) or even desirable (when the long-range goals become rigid; people who have reached childhood goals and hold to them without further search are spiritually dead).

Five Areas of Meaning

The most practical help a counselor can provide is to lead us to circumstances in which we are likely to find meaning. There are at least five such circumstances.

The first is situations in which we discover a truth about ourselves. The insight may be triggered by an experience or by something seen, heard, read, fantasized, or dreamed about; but the discovery must be ours. We must say to ourselves, "Yes, that's the way I am. That's how I feel, think, react; these are my strong points, these are my shortcomings; this is what I like about myself, and this is what I'd like to change." From childhood on we are prompted to put on masks to please, to hide real or imagined weakness, to protect ourselves from rejection. Often we accept the mask for our true self. A peek under our masks will give us a sense of meaning. That can happen in meditation, in reading the thoughts of wise men and women, by experiencing the works of artists or the beauty of nature, through creative activities, and in honest encounters with others.

The second circumstance in which meanings become apparent concerns situations in which we see choices, limited as they may be. Despair comes from a sense of feeling trapped. Logotherapy maintains that we have choices under all circumstances, choices about the things we can change and choices about our attitudes regarding those we cannot change. We may be trapped, but we are not without choice. We can decide to give up, feel sorry for ourselves, storm against an unchangeable situation, or ask ourselves what we, even in this hopeless situation, still can do. The conditions do not determine a person, says Frankl, but "he determines himself whether to give in to conditions or to stand up to them" (*MS*, p. 206).*

The logotherapist makes us aware of a choice of attitudes, which in turn opens up meanings in situations of unavoidable suffering that in itself is meaningless. The logotherapist helps us find options; but once we see alternatives, we are likely to find a way out. Even if all escape routes are blocked, suffering may reveal a meaning, sometimes much

* Throughout, references to Frankl's books are identified parenthetically by abbreviated title. For an explanation of abbreviations, see p. 171.

later. One client said, "The meaning of suffering is that it changes you for the better." Growth, maturing, and understanding are often the long-range results of suffering. One aspect of finding meaning through attitudinal choice concerns the past. We cannot change the facts of our past, remove childhood traumas, undo mistakes, or change our early environment. Our choice consists of either letting the past drag us down or learning from the experience. We can use childhood traumas as excuses for present failures or as challenges to be overcome.

The third circumstance where meaning reveals itself is one in which we experience our uniqueness. When we feel replaceable—in a job or a relationship—life seems meaningless. We may feel replaceable as a worker, voter, consumer, even as a spouse or parent; but there are areas where we are unique. Two such areas are personal relationships and artistic activities. Only *we* relate to an offspring, a spouse, or a friend in the way we do; only *we* make a poem, a painting, a collage in exactly the manner we create it. Here we are irreplaceable.

The last two circumstances in which meaning can be found are less comfortable. They require responsibleness (Chapter VIII) and "self-transcendence," a concept central in Frankl's thinking (Chapter X). We all like to find out the truth about ourselves, make choices, and feel unique. But the freedom of making choices will not lead to a meaningful life if it is not lived responsibly and only for one's own sake. Responsibility presupposes a demand quality in life to which we have to respond and which requires transcending our self-centeredness. We may conceive these demands as coming from God (if we are religiously inclined) or from life (if our world view is secular); but the result is the same. The questions "Who am I?" and "What are my goals?" in order to yield meaningful answers take on the sense of "Who ought I to be?" "What are my potentials?" "How can I do not merely fit into life but improve it?"

Ordinarily, the answers to such questions come from time-tested values passed from generation to generation. Values, defined by Frankl as "universal meaning" (*UG*, pp. 119–120), under normal circumstances provide useful guidelines toward meaning. But, as discussed in Chapter VII, we have occasionally to supplement, perhaps replace, general values by our personal response to the specific meaning demands of the moment. This is especially true in times like the present, when traditional values undergo vast and rapid change. For instance, the idea of war as a noble enterprise has to be reexamined in a world of nuclear weapons; the benefits of a large family need reappraisal in a world threatened by population expansion; the blessings of ever-expanding production must be reevaluated in a world facing pollution and the exploitation of nonrenewable resources; and in a technological affluent society a second look has to be taken at the value of work as contrasted to leisure as sources of meaning. Such unprecedented changes require that we choose with a sense of responsibleness.

But even responsible decisions will not fill the existential vacuum if we make them only for our own sake. Meaning comes from commitments that transcend personal interests; it comes, as Frankl puts it, from "reaching beyond the self toward causes to serve or people to love " (*UC*, p. 35). Those who are religious in a traditional sense find meaning by acting for the sake of God. Those whose search for meaning is secular will find it by acting for the sake of another human being or for a cause. Most people want to be free, unique, and self-reliant; but most of all they want to be useful, to know for whom or for what they live, work, suffer, and die.

We Are Healthier than We Think

Many older therapies place responsibility for our difficulties on our early upbringing. Logotherapy is "education to responsibility." Outside influences are important but not all-determining. Within limitations we have a say about who we are and who we want to become. We need never let ourselves be reduced to helpless victims. Consequently, logotherapy—unlike therapies that aim at equilibrium by adjusting patients to society—does not see a tensionless life as a therapeutic goal. Tension is part of living as a human being in a human society. To remain healthy, the unhealthy tensions of body and psyche are to be avoided. But the healthy tension of the spirit strengthens our spiritual muscles. The healthiest tension is between what we are and what we have the vision of growing toward, or, to use Frankl's favorite phrase, "the tension between being and meaning" (*PE*, p. 10).

The struggle for meaning is not easy. Life does not owe us pleasure; it does offer us meaning. Mental health does not come to those who demand happiness but to those who find meanings; to them happiness comes as a side product. "It must *en*sue," says Frankl. "It cannot be *pur*sued" (*UG*, p. 85).

Logotherapy maintains and restores mental health by providing a sound view of the human being and the world as we know it. It draws on the huge reservoir of health stored in our specifically human dimension—our creativity, capacity to love, outreach, desire to be useful, goal orientation, and will to meaning. Logophilosophy emphasizes what is *right* with us, what we like about ourself, our accomplishments, and our peak experiences. It also considers the qualities we dislike so we may change them, our failures so we can learn from them, our abysses so we may lift ourselves up, knowing that peaks exist and can be reached.

Logophilosophy itself is therapeutic—curing and preventing. How it is translated into therapy proper is discussed in Chapter IX. The special methods of logotherapy are the Socratic dialogue, paradoxical intention, and dereflection. The therapist uses them to bring about a change of attitude and to open avenues for a search in which the clients have the major responsibility but in which the therapist plays an active part. Logotherapy provides the tools for our pursuit of meaning, keeping dependency on the therapist at a minimum.

1. Personal Discovery

As long as a man has a dream in his head, he cannot lose the significance of living.

HOWARD THURMAN

At the age of twenty-eight and after a sheltered middle-class life in Vienna, I found myself in a camp for vagabonds in Belgium. The other inmates were mostly professional people—civil servants, attorneys, businessmen, and one or two professors. We were vagabonds only because we had entered Belgium without a visa, after having been disenfranchised as human beings by the Nazis in our native Austria. The year was 1938.

We slept in dormitories, in groups of forty. Printed along the walls above the steel-framed cots were quotations reflecting the wisdom of the ages: "Honesty is the best policy." "Be good and you will be rewarded." "Work by the sweat of your brow, and you will harvest the riches." One sixty-year-old refugee, who had been a judge for half his life, took an overdose of sleeping pills under a sign that said, "Do justice, and justice will be done to you." Here on the walls of the vagabond dormitory I came face to face with a double standard for the meaning of life—first as it must be lived in the presence of misery, insecurity, and apparent senselessness, and second as it is presented by the lawmakers who write the moral codes—life's meaning as we experience it versus life's meaning as humanity thinks it ought to be.

I had met this dilemma before. As a law student at the University of Vienna I had come to realize that all the thousands of rules regulating our lives were based originally on brilliantly conceived answers to human needs but that once codified they offered words instead of compassion. As an attorney's apprentice I had to raid the apartments of people who were behind in their rent and seize any valuables I could find. Early one morning I had an experience that eventually made me give up my law career. My victim, an old man in a long nightgown, fell to his knees and begged me, the twenty-three-year-old upholder of law and order, to leave him his watch, his last family heirloom. The officer of the court who was with me insisted that the law left me no choice but to seize the watch.

Some other early experiences had convinced me how easily religion, too, can be taken over by the lawmakers. Early prophets' insights into human spiritual yearnings had been codified into customs and rituals. I found examples among Christian neighbors and Jewish friends. They observed the religious laws down to the finest points. A lady from a devoutly orthodox Jewish family, the owner of a hotel in an Austrian mountain resort, went to town late on Friday afternoon. On her way back she met the mailman, who, trying to save himself a climb, handed her a stack of mail for her hotel guests. When she started up the hill, she noted the first star, heralding the Sabbath. Because the talmudic laws forbid the carrying of packages on the Sabbath, she put the mail for her eighty guests on the sidewalk and went home. My young mind misinterpreted such stories as demonstrating that religion was ridiculous and meaningless. Only years later did I realize it is the laws, customs, and rituals that make one person ridicule, look down upon, and eventually hate another person's religion. The true meanings of our beliefs are never laughable. True beliefs unite us; desperate efforts to preserve those beliefs tear us apart.

I grew up in a city where religion had come to mean blaming the Jews for all evils, from the death of Jesus to unemployment. It always struck me as bitter irony that the Jews, who had been the first with enough imagination to replace human sacrifice with sacrificial goats, themselves had become the scapegoats.

I remember my mood of rebellion in that camp for vagabonds. Why did this happen to me? Did I deserve my suffering because of some hidden fault of which I was not aware? Was there no order or justice? Was everything mere chance, whim, and chaos? I remember my intense desire—in fact, my demand—for an answer. The response was a vast silence. While evil and injustice triumphed, some of my friends found comfort in a religion that had meant little to them in more fortunate times. One remark made by a schoolmate I later met again in New York sticks in my memory: "If I didn't think that there was some meaning behind it all, I'd kill myself."

I wanted to believe in meaning, in a plan designed by a great and just architect; but it proved difficult. My father had been shipped to a concentration camp immediately after an operation and had died in a cattle wagon. My mother, the gentlest person imaginable, who never knowingly had done harm to anyone, was with him and literally died of a broken heart. I rebelled. I rejected. I still was the lawyer arguing logical rebuttals. Where was the meaning of it all?

By the end of the forties my law career had faded into the past. I had been forced to live life, not study its case histories. Having learned a new language, I had found my way back to an earlier interest in writing and editing. And it gradually dawned on me that God was not merely a lawgiver but also a creative author and editor. Possibly He created in ways different from those of human authors, who plan a story and then write according to the outline. Was it not possible that the world was designed by constant editing rather than by writing according to a plan—by hindsight rather than foresight? Humans had not been created like a carefully plotted story; they had come into existence only after infinite experimentation that had also produced the tubercle bacillus, the dodo, and the giraffe. By human standards this seems a slow and wasteful type of authorship, but for the creative force that knows no limitations of time it may have been the best. Perhaps life, too, was continuously created by constant experimentation; and perhaps we, the creatures, followed this same pattern of creation—not able to see ahead but forced to find our direction from looking backward at past experiences. Here was the possibility of a plan in the midst of apparent chaos, of meaning in the midst of meaninglessness.

The time of emigration was full of self-doubt and groping; and if a psychiatrist (or anyone else) had told me that this painful fumbling contained an element of good, I would have rejected the notion. Yet as it turned out the painful search turned a boy into a man. The Austrian writer Stefan Zweig, having suffered so much during his exile that he committed suicide in South America, had the perception to maintain that emigration is good for those who survive it. This can be said of any suffering. From suffering can come meaning.

Then one Sunday morning, quite by accident, I wandered into the Unitarian Church of Berkeley and heard a minister, in full ministerial robes and from a pulpit, preach a sermon: No one can ever know the true nature of God; all concepts of God are human concepts; we all must work out the concept that confirms our own life experience; but underlying each person's beliefs must be that deep conviction that we are not alone, that we are not the victims of mere chance, that it does make a difference how we conduct ourselves, that we do have a place in the scheme of things. It was comforting, following this experience, to spend many evenings with people engaged in a busy search for a personal belief. God was seen in many ways: as perfection, ultimate concern, heart of the universe, an evolving force, a father, a co-creator with human beings. I did not know it then, but this was group therapy, a great healing process.

The healing did not come about through finding new answers but through asking new questions. The question "Why did it happen to me?" remained unanswerable; and to insist on an answer led only to anguish and, worse, to fatalism. It led to the belief that because injustice and chance exist, all efforts are hopeless and there is no point in even trying. But when the question was phrased differently, the same situation that had been senseless became a challenge: "Granted that there are chance and injustice in the world, what can I—and sometimes only I—do in the situation in which I find myself?"

Again there were doubts. Was I merely rationalizing, fooling myself into seeing relevance where there was nothing but emptiness? Then, and again by accident, I read Viktor Frankl's *Man's Search for Meaning* and later met the author in San Francisco. Once more I had the satisfaction of having my personal gropings justified by a "professional"— a psychiatrist this time, and a professor of my own alma mater, the University of Vienna. In the books and pamphlets he sent me I found a scholarly world view that made each of us responsible for finding our own life's meaning as a prerequisite to mental health.

I accompanied Frankl on his lecture tours in California, visited him in Vienna, and followed people's reactions to his message. I have been moved to see how many persons feel as lonely, bewildered, frustrated, and empty as I had felt after my expulsion and how desperately they are seeking a way out of the meaninglessness of their own lives. If Hitlerism was a breakdown of values and traditions, the same breakdown has now occurred in many places and under many names, even under the name of progress and affluence. And once a person experiences expulsion from whatever paradise and from whatever security, he or she is left to grope for meaning and order.

Logotherapy, Frankl's method of curing mental illness, also contains a philosophy that can help people retain their sanity. William S. Sahakian, professor of philosophy at Suffolk University, once said, "Frankl has put man in his proper place in the scheme of things, by making a human being out of him instead of reducing him, as reductionism does, to the animal level. He has restored cosmos in our thinking in place of chaos, order out of disorder, meaning out of non-sense. Finally, he is restoring sanity, in the sense that he has implanted meaningfulness in place of meaninglessness, optimism in place of pessimism and cynicism, rationality in place of irrationality."[1]

In this book I have attempted to relate this philosophy to the American scene. *The Pursuit of Meaning* may be read intellectually or existentially. One may read it for the information it contains or for its impact on one's own life. One may ask, "What can I learn from it in the way of general knowledge?" or "What does it mean to me personally? How does it relate to my work, to my experience with other people, to the sufferings I have gone through, to the decisions I make, to my search for values and meanings, to the way I pursue happiness, to what I expect of life, and to how I take disappointment?"

This book presents Frankl's views on meaning in a world where the old guidelines of general values and traditions are fading and we are forced to search for our own. Accordingly, we will make our own personal discoveries in the ideas here offered. What I gained from logotherapy is the recognition that central to human life is the pursuit of meaning and not the pursuit of happiness, that we only invite frustration if we expect life to be primarily pleasurable, that life imposes obligations, and that pleasure and happiness come from responding to the tasks of life. I also realized through logotherapy that when the going is tough and nothing makes sense, throwing out religion solves no problem. In times of despair and doubt we will have to search for a "religion" in the broadest sense of the word, a meaning that makes sense to us in our particular situation. It may be the religion of our childhood or some other established creed, but our search may also lead us outside existing religions.

Logotherapy taught me that this search is personal (although it can be carried on in groups) and that we all must engage in it even though we never can be certain we are on the right track or what exactly our goal is. We undertake this search in the face of ultimate uncertainty. Finally, I achieved through logotherapy the belief that we must take life one step at a time, that we must not look for the grandiose plan but for the challenges of the moment. With luck we will get an occasional glimpse of the grandiose plan. The important thing is to assume it exists.

The Beginnings of Logotherapy

Viktor Frankl was born in Vienna in 1905. From his childhood he sensed a depth to life that went beyond material comfort. His earliest recollection is that of waking up one morning with a strong feeling of peace and security. When he opened his eyes, he saw his father standing over him, calmly watching him. He also remembers as a child sitting up one night, struck by the idea that he, like everyone else, some day would die. In school he baffled his teachers by bringing up precocious questions. When he was fourteen his science teacher explained that life in the last analysis was nothing but a process of combustion. The boy startled the class by jumping to his feet, shouting, "If that is so, then what meaning does life have?" (*PE*, p. 20). When another student from his high school was found dead, a suicide, with a book of nihilistic writings in his hand, Frankl realized the close connection between philosophical concepts and actual life. It confirmed his opposition to nihilism, the belief in nonmeaning that, he became convinced, was the root of despair and cruelty. The atrocities of the death camps, he maintains, were not invented in Nazi offices but in the writings of nihilistic philosophers.

Before he finished high school Frankl had begun a scientific correspondence with Sigmund Freud that led to the publication of one of Frankl's papers in Freud's *International Journal of Psychoanalysis*. As a medical student Frankl became a member of the inner circle of Alfred Adler, the founder of individual psychology, but gradually moved away from the orthodox Adlerian view, which led to Frankl's eventual exclusion from the Adlerian Society in Vienna.

The young student became increasingly dissatisfied with the narrowness of the psychiatric orientation around him. While crediting Freud with finding new insights into human nature, Frankl felt that within the circle of Viennese psychoanalysis Freud's ideas, like so many great ideas, had begun to harden into rigid concepts. What was needed was to understand the human being in his or her totality, and Frankl set out on a career in psychiatry in which he introduced the concepts of meanings and values into psychiatric thought. "At that point," he recalled later, "I suspended what I had learned from my great teachers and began listening to what my patients were telling me—trying to learn from them."[2]

He found many opportunities to listen to patients. After receiving his M.D. degree in 1930, he worked at the neuropsychiatric clinic of the University of Vienna, where Freud and the only Nobel Prize winner in psychiatry, Julius von Wagner-Jauregg, gave their lectures and where Manfred Sakel developed his insulin shock therapy. In addition to his work at the university, Frankl founded youth counseling centers. Here the fundamental formulations of logotherapy took shape: that all reality has meaning *(logos)* and that life never ceases to have meaning for anyone; that meaning is very specific and changes from person to person and for each person from moment to moment; that each person is unique and each life contains a series of unique demands that have to be discovered and responded to; that the response to these provides meaning; and that happiness, contentment, peace of mind, and self-actualization are mere side products in the search for meaning.

Many patients in the youth centers were in despair because they could not find jobs in those years of economic depression. Frankl discovered that giving them a task to fulfill, such as organizing and participating in youth meetings, relieved their despair, even though these were unpaid jobs. Despair, Frankl decided, was suffering behind which the sufferer could see no meaning. But meaning can be found in a much wider range than the sufferer realizes, and it is the task of the therapist to widen the patient's horizon, to expose the patient to the full range of meaning possibilities. Most of those who came to the youth centers contemplating suicide saw the meaning of their lives in one direction only—the unemployed in getting work, the unmarried in finding a spouse, and the barren in having a child. Then there were those who saw no meaning anywhere, who simply felt empty and could not bear an empty life. To explore this phenomenon of inner emptiness—the "existential vacuum," as he termed it—became the meaning of Frankl's life during the depression years in a politically unstable republican Austria that clung to the dreams of old monarchic glory. He helped his patients find perspective; rise above their narrow, selfish interests; and find meaning in their activities, paid or unpaid, and in their relationships with others. Above all, meaning could be found in accepting the unavoidable and by doing so turning it into a challenge. History is full of examples supporting this view: a stutterer may give up or become a Demosthenes; a blind deaf-mute may despair or become a Helen Keller; a polio cripple may withdraw from life or become president of the United States.

Trial by Holocaust

Frankl's paradise, too, ended in expulsion; but the cherubim with the fiery swords wore brown shirts with swastika armbands. In the introduction to his still untranslated book, *Homo Patiens*, he quotes Friedrich Nietzsche: "Not the suffering itself was his problem but that the answer was wanting to the outcry, 'Why the suffering?'" In the death camp, the question of "Why did this happen to me?" was bound to end in frustrated despair because no answer existed, at least not on the human level. But if the victims were able to see the holocaust as something they were forced to endure, however undeservedly, if they were able to say to themselves, "All right—it happened; what can I do now?" there was at least some measure of hope to go forward on. The hope was survival but not for survival's sake alone. It was survival for the sake of a task, what one intended to do with the life that was preserved: to be reunited with a wife, to bring up a child, to finish a book, or simply to flee and help fight Nazism. Survival contained a task behind which, perhaps unconsciously, stood the belief that some kind of order still prevailed and that one could reach for it even while braving the chaos.

Such was Frankl's message, which he later expressed in his writings and which helped him to survive. It is a valid message for any situation. If we think of ourselves as helpless pieces of debris tossed about in a wild ocean, we are likely to give up and drown. But if we see ourselves as human beings, although shipwrecked, we will discover choices, however minute, that can make a difference.

Frankl's expulsion took the grim form of two and a half years in German concentration camps. The manuscript of the book that was to announce the message of logotherapy (which later was published as *The Doctor and the Soul*) was lost and had to be rewritten after his camp experiences had confirmed his theories. The manuscript was gone, his family had been killed, and Frankl's own life seemed destroyed. But his theories postulated that life never ceases to have meaning. "The concentration camps served as a crucible to test the validity of logotherapy," he told students at the United States International University in San Diego, where he teaches during winter quarters. "The lesson to learn from Auschwitz was that man is a being in search for meaning. If there is anything to uphold him even in such an extreme situation, it is the awareness that life has a meaning to fulfill, albeit in the future. The message of Auschwitz is: human existence is dependent on self-transcendence, survival is dependent on direction. And I think this is true not only of the survival of individuals but also for the survival of mankind."[3]

It is true that in the death camps survival depended on more than one's meaning orientation (for instance, on the whims of an SS guard). But by and large those inmates who saw meaning potentials even in their desperate situation had a greater chance to survive. Frankl conquered the despair that caused the death of many his fellow inmates by asking himself "Does the meaning of my life really depend on the publication of a manuscript, even if it contains the work of my entire life up to now?" He turned to other meaning potentials that still were open to him. He organized an information network that notified him of anyone who showed suicidal intentions. Although he was required to do hard labor up to eighteen hours a day and his weight was at one point reduced to eighty pounds, he continued his profession of counseling. In one of the four camps in which he was imprisoned he even gathered around him a group of inmates who were, as he was himself, enthusiastic rock climbers. They met every two weeks and one of them recalled some rock-climbing exploits in the Alps. Engrossed in listening, in their own memories, and in their hope of seeing their mountains again, they were able to rise above their hopeless situation for a few moments at least.

Frankl's confinement in the concentration camps convinced him more than ever that each person is a unique individual who can retain a last reserve of freedom to take a stand, at least inwardly, even under the most restrictive circumstances. This seemed a painful and drastic experiment to disprove Freud's contention that when one takes different individuals and starves them, their differences are blotted out. Yet in the camps some inmates degenerated into animals fighting for survival while a few attained virtual sainthood by helping their fellow victims. "Hunger," Frankl recalls, "revealed their true selves. To quote the title of a bestseller: 'Calories don't count'" (*UC*, p. 48).

His experiences in the camps confirmed Frankl's belief in a dimension in which we not only *are* but in each moment can decide what we are going to *become*. The lessons learned in Auschwitz are summarized in his conviction that even when we are stripped of everything we *have*—family, friends, influence, status, possessions—no one can take from us the freedom to make our decision of what we are to become because this freedom is not something we *have* but something we *are*. To this dimension of freedom we must turn in our existential despair, and to this the logotherapist must direct the patient's attention.

Frankl returned to Vienna, a city of despair after the wartime destruction, that was swarming with Austrian Nazis.

To stay there and help, he decided, was his special assignment. It was not easy to make this decision in the face of what had happened to him and his immediate family (except for one sister, all members had been killed). But he stuck to his belief that each individual must be judged on his or her own merits, that to condemn a group wholesale as if it were a factory lot of defective shoes is to dehumanize people, to treat them as things, whether they be Jews or Nazis. He was convinced all persons have the power and the freedom to rise above their former selves and become different, better. But even he was amazed at a dramatic example that came to his attention after the war.

"Let me cite the case of Dr. J.," Frankl recalls in *Man's Search for Meaning* (pp. 207-208). "He was the only man I ever encountered in my whole life whom I would dare to call a Mephistophelean being, a satanic figure. At that time he was generally called 'the mass murderer of Steinhof,' the name of the large mental hospital in Vienna. When the Nazis started their euthanasia program, he held all the strings in his hands and was so fanatic in the job assigned to him that he tried not to let one single psychotic individual escape the gas chamber." After the war Frankl learned that Dr. J. apparently had escaped. Years later he met a former Austrian diplomat who had been imprisoned in Siberia and then in the Ljubljanka prison in Moscow, who "suddenly asked me whether I happened to know Dr. J. After my affirmative reply he continued: I made his acquaintance in Ljubljanka. There he died, at about forty, from cancer of the urinary bladder. Before he died, however, he showed himself to be the best comrade you can imagine! He gave consolation to everybody. He lived up to the highest conceivable moral standard. He was the best friend I ever met during my long years in prison!'" This episode showed Frankl that even in this dramatic instance he would have made a tragic mistake if he had drawn his conclusion from what seemed to be an incarnation of the satanic principle, and had denied Dr. J. the capacity to change for the better.

For Frankl the postwar years were most creative. Within fourteen years he published fourteen books. He became the head of the department of neurology at the Vienna Poliklinik Hospital and professor of psychiatry at the University of Vienna. As the founder of logotherapy he received from the Austrian president the Medal of Honor First Class for Science and Art and from Vienna's mayor the Natural Science Award of the city of Vienna. He has been on some fifty lecture tours in the United States, lecturing in one hundred and fifty universities and colleges. He has been a visiting professor at Harvard, Southern Methodist, Stanford, and Duquesne universities and received honorary doctorates from Loyola University (Chicago), Edgecliff College (Cincinnati), and Rockford College (Illinois). At the United States International University in San Diego, California, he serves part of the year as distinguished professor of logotherapy.

His books, numbering twenty-three by now, have been translated into seventeen languages. Six are available in English, but there is no book in any language that summarizes Frankl's ideas in nontechnical language. Many of his German books are either medical or philosophical, and he is one of those academicians who believes science simplified is science falsified.

This book is an attempt to build bridges, to simplify without oversimplifying. It is not written as a handbook for therapists or as a do-it-yourself book for patients. It is written for the millions of people who are healthy but believe they are sick because they feel empty; for those who are looking for meaning in frantic activity, money, power, speed, excitement, sex, alcohol, drugs, or the pursuit of happiness for its own sake. We all have been expelled from our own paradise and lived through our own concentration camp. To help people endure has always been the task of the prophets and priests and philosophers and educators. Now they are joined by the psychologists, psychiatrists, and other "helping professions." Logotherapy supplies one contemporary answer to the age-old problem of how to live after the expulsion and how to find meaning during and after the trials of suffering.

2. The Human Dimension

Man is an animal that makes promises to himself.

FRIEDRICH NIETZSCHE

Logotherapy is therapy through meaning. The dictionary translation of the Greek word *logos* is "the controlling principle of the universe" or, in theological terms, "the word (or will) of God." Frankl translates *logos* as "meaning." If his translation is accepted, then meaning is the controlling principle of the universe; it is at the center of life toward which we all move, consciously or unconsciously. To Frankl our basic motivation for living is not to find pleasure, power, or material riches but to find meaning. Pleasure, an important component of happiness, is merely a by-product of having found meaning. Power and material goods contribute to our well-being but are simply means to an end, to be used in a meaningful way. Meaning is neither a by-product nor a means. It is an end in itself.

Logotherapy is more than therapy. It is logophilosophy, a view about ourselves and our place in life that will help us make sense of our life in spite of its tragedies. Many people who have learned about logophilosophy have expressed amazement that they have used it in bits and pieces without knowing anything about logotherapy. In a letter Frankl received recently a woman wrote, "I believe in logotherapy because it worked after I tried it on myself, and I had read about it in only one single book." Logophilosophy puts into a holistic system much of the wisdom of the ages, common sense, and the findings of modern psychology. It can be the basis of self-therapy as well as counseling.

Logotherapy also takes the form of education. It strengthens our assurance that we have choices, that we are unique, that we have the power to defy limitations by overcoming them or changing our attitudes where they cannot be overcome. Logoeducation teaches us to become independent (even from the therapist) and to take responsibility for our decisions. It counteracts the prevailing tendency to reduce ourselves to a mere animal that can be trained or a machine that can be manipulated. It reinforces our innate inclination toward self-transcendence.

Logotherapy also can be logoministry, in cases where we are called upon to minister to someone in crisis situations either as a professional to a patient or as a layperson to a friend or relative.

Logotherapy, as therapy, can be curative and preventive, primary and supplementary. It can cure neuroses that originated in the human spirit and strengthen spiritual muscles. It can be applied directly or be combined with other forms of psychotherapy and with pharmacology.

Basic Assumptions of Logotherapy

Like all therapies, logotherapy is based on certain assumptions about human nature and our place in the universe. Its basic assumption is that in addition to our physical and psychological dimensions we possess a specifically human dimension of the spirit, and all three must be considered if we are to be fully understood. Our human dimension enables us to reach beyond ourselves and to make meanings and values an essential part of our existence. Life has meaning under all, even the most miserable, conditions; we possess a deeply rooted conscience that helps us find the specific meanings of our unique life.

Our main motivation for living is not seeking pleasure but self-chosen tasks, and the deepest pleasure comes from accomplishing these tasks. We are seen as free agents—not always able to free ourselves from limitations, but always free to take a stand within and even against our limitations. We are free to make choices regarding our activities, experiences, and attitudes; but to be meaningful they must not be made arbitrarily but rather be tempered by responsibility.

Logotherapy also asserts that each person is unique, going through a lifelong series of unique, unrepeatable moments, each offering a meaning potential. To recognize these offerings and to be able to respond to them, is to lead a "response-able," meaningful life.

These assumptions will be discussed and illustrated in later chapters. Most basic is the assumption that the human being is an entity consisting of body, psyche, and spirit. Sigmund Freud added a new dimension to the understanding of ourselves and our diseases when he discovered that sickness originates not only in the body but also in the psyche. Viktor Frankl adds another dimension, the human spirit. Sickness originates not only in body and psyche but in our spirit. As we will see, our spirit supplies the resources through which health may be restored and maintained. The human spirit, of course, is not a new concept. It always has been important in religious imagery. What is new is that logotherapy sees the human spirit in medical terms, as a source of health. Before Freud, says Frankl, medicine disregarded the human psyche; it still largely disregards the human spirit.

To understand logotherapy, it is important to know what is meant by the human spirit. It is not restricted to the religious; everyone has a spirit, those in the Judeo-Christian tradition, believers in Eastern religions, as well as atheists, agnostics, and humanists. To get away from religious connotations, Frankl calls the human spirit also the "noëtic" dimension. The term is taken from the Greek *noös* or mind. But Frankl uses the term to include everything that is specifically human. The noëtic (spiritual, specifically human) dimension contains such qualities as our will to meaning, our goal orientation, ideas and ideals, creativity, imagination, faith, love that goes beyond the physical, a conscience beyond the superego, self-transcendence, commitments, responsibility, a sense of humor, and the freedom of choice making. The human dimension is the medicine chest of the logotherapist. Patients are made aware that they have these rich resources of health within. The spirit may be blocked by physical or psychological illness, which may have to be cured by traditional medical means before logotherapy proper can be applied.

While it is easy to distinguish our physical aspects from the instinctual and the spiritual, many people find it difficult to separate the latter two. Instinctual acts are done because we are driven, a response to a "need." The motivations for our instinctual acts are pleasure, power, and prestige. We act for self-actualization. For our spiritual acts we are the drivers; we make the decisions, take the responsibility, and accept the commitments. We respond to personal choice. The motivation for our spiritual acts is meaning. We act for self-transcendence, for the sake of someone or something beyond ourselves.

Frankl explains the dimension of the spirit with a simile: an airplane acts like a car as long as it taxies on the ground; its true nature becomes apparent only when it lifts into the air, into three-dimensional space. Similarly, the human being is an animal. But we are much more, an entire dimension more, than an animal. Only when we lift ourselves into the dimension of spirit do we become fully human. To Frankl the human dimension is the dimension of freedom: "Not the freedom from conditions" (*PE*, p. 75), be they biological, psychological, or sociological (*PE*, p. 60); not the freedom *from* anything, but the freedom *to* something, "the freedom to take a stand toward conditions" *(PE,* p. 75). Thus we become truly human only when we lift ourselves into the dimension of freedom.

In the dimension of body we are imprisoned; in the dimension of psyche we are driven; but in the dimension of spirit we are free. Here we do not merely exist; we can influence our existence. We can decide not only what kind of person we are but what kind of person we still can become. In the noëtic dimension we are the choice makers. Only neurotics, Frankl tells his students, misunderstand their existence as "This is the way I have to be." Healthy persons have the attitude of "I can always change."

A Three-Dimensional Entity

Logotherapy does not see the human being as "composed" of body, psyche, and spirit as if they were parts of a whole. The person is seen as a unity, and to emphasize this oneness Frankl speaks of the "dimensions of human existence." Just as we have a length, breadth, and height that are inseparable, so our body, psyche, and spirit are three inseparable dimensions. If one is disregarded, we do not get a full human being but a shadow, a two-dimensional projection. Look at a circle, he says, in a two-dimensional plane. You cannot tell if it is the projection of a sphere, a cylinder, or a cone. To know the true character of the geometric body, you must look at its three-dimensional reality of body, psyche, and spirit. Disregard the spirit (which is still widely done in medicine), and you get a shadow, a caricature, an automaton of reflexes, a helpless victim of reactions and instincts, a product of drives, heredity, and environment.

When doctors look at a patient, disregarding the noëtic dimension, they may see a schizophrenic who hallucinates and hears voices. True enough. But the patient is much more. In his lecture at Columbia University Frankl explained, "If I project a person like Fëdor Dostoevski or Bernadette Soubirous into the psychiatric plane, then Dostoevski for me is nothing but an epileptic, and Bernadette nothing but a hysteric with visionary hallucinations. What they are beyond that I cannot see in the psychiatric plane. Artistic achievements and religious encounters go beyond the psychiatric plane."[1] All pathology, he told the students, requires first of all a diagnosis, a "looking through," namely a looking through the *pathos* at the *logos* which lies beyond it, a looking through the suffering at the meaning behind it.

To disregard the spiritual dimension is reductionism, which Frankl considers at the root of our malaise of feeling empty and that life is devoid of meaning. In *Homo Patiens* he wrote as early as 1950: "If we consider man merely as a machine ruled by conditioned reflexes, then anthropology is degraded to an annex of zoology, and the ontology of man becomes the doctrine of certain animals whose ability to walk on their hind legs has gone to their heads."

The danger of such reductionism has never been greater than it is today. The biological sciences have discovered that indeed we are "programmed" by our genetic setup and determined by our glandular functions, chemical reactions, and electrical charges. The social sciences are telling us we are the product of social and economic forces that move us about like pawns in a chess game. And psychology informs us about the drives and instincts that push us around whether we want it or not and about the various conditioning processes that determine our behavior. Frankl does not agree with Freud's statement that we do not live but "are lived" by our instincts. Such fatalism, based on scientific thinking, is responsible for some of the dead ends in which we find ourselves.

As an existential philosopher, Frankl explores existence

from the point of view of personal experience. He starts out, as do all existential philosophers, with Descartes's *sum*, the "I am." To Frankl the *sum* is not a biologically determined being, as Darwin understood it, or a sociologically determined being, as Marx believed, or a psychologically determined being, as Freud thought. To Frankl, human beings, while determined in all these ways, retain an important area of freedom where they are not determined at all but are free to take a stand. In *Logos und Existenz* he gives some contemporary examples of where this determinism can lead. Racism, for instance, uses biology to tell people they are predetermined. Hitler told the German people they were determined by their biology, by their "blood," and nothing could be done about it. If you were a Jew, you were judged not on the grounds of your social or intellectual contributions, but merely on the grounds of biology. In Marxism it is only the sociological environment that counts. You are judged on the basis of being capitalist or proletarian. And in the United States the tendency has developed to regard people as the outcome of their unconscious dynamics. Freud's views are in danger of becoming dogma in the United States, as Hitler's were dogma in Germany and Marx's are dogma in the Communist countries. The racist is certain that only our biology determines us; the Marxist is just as certain that our behavior is determined by class and environment; and the popularization and misunderstanding of Freud's ideas have convinced many Americans we are determined by drives and instincts and thus can be manipulated by "hidden persuaders." This has led to a fatalism in patients that is difficult to overcome. A young girl, for instance, in defending her tendency to give up too easily, her readiness to throw away her life, told Frankl: "What can I do, doctor? I'm just a typical only child according to Alfred Adler." To her this meant that no one could help her, and least of all could she help herself, because she was stuck with unchangeable traits.

Frankl does not deny that biological, social, and psychological forces exert great influence; but as he once phrased it in a filmed interview with Huston Smith, professor of philosophy at MIT, "Man is determined, but never pandetermined." Frankl has always maintained that even under the most restrictive circumstances we have an area in which we can determine our actions, our experiences, or at least our attitudes; and this freedom of self-determination rests in our noëtic realm.

The Freedom to Change

Our freedom gives us the opportunity to change, to step away from ourselves, even to confront ourselves. Our noëtic self, concerned with other beings to love and meanings to fulfill, can face our physical and psychological organism in a confrontation that can bring about changes in attitudes. Logotherapy underlines "the defiant power of the human spirit" (PE, p. 99) that enables us to resist the forces of environment and instinct and allows us to rise above any condition that fate may inflict on us.

That the defiant power of the spirit is more than a phrase became evident to me when I accompanied Frankl to San Quentin Prison in California, where he gave a talk to the inmates. The turnout was disappointing. Only about fifty of the more than three thousand prisoners had assembled in the chapel, and they were not at all a captive audience. Some left during Frankl's introduction. Others seemed withdrawn and hostile. They perked up when he told about his death camp experiences. They became attentive when he talked about the despair of prison life. These were the toughest criminals in California, many of them repeaters, but their faces stirred with emotion when Frankl told them it is never too late, not to their last breath, to change their attitudes not only toward their fate but also toward themselves—they were not "born losers" hopelessly entangled in evil. "It lies in your power," he told them "to step away from your former, guilty self, regardless of what happened to you in your life." A huge black man later remarked, "He never mentioned God. He said I have it in myself to change, and maybe he is right. He's gone through it; he ought to know." Another prisoner said, "They always treat us as hopeless criminals or as psychopaths, here in prison and also outside, and so we eventually give up trying—what's the use?" A third said, "The psychologists always ask us about our childhood and the bad things in the past. Always the past—it's like a millstone around our necks. But he [Frankl] talked about what we still can do, even in prison." And then he added, "Most of us don't even come any more to hear psychologists speak. I only came because I read that he'd been a prisoner, too."[2]

This episode does not prove that Frankl's concepts are true but merely that his approach to truth speaks to people today, even if they have been economically deprived, psychologically twisted, and socially rebuffed. It was a new thought for the prisoners in San Quentin that in spite of their obvious handicaps it was still in their power to influence their fate, even if ever so slightly, to make a fresh start, to disassociate themselves from many aspects they had come to consider as millstones around their necks. And the appeal was all the stronger because such a "miracle of conversion" was possible outside the channels of religion, which some of the prisoners considered meaningless at best and tools of the hated establishment at worst. A spiritual uplifting, or one might call it a "noëtic uplifting," took place independent of traditional religion.

The effects of the visit were also indicated in a letter Frankl received from an inmate, the editor of the prison newspaper, *San Quentin News*. The man had written up Frankl's visit, and the article later received first place in a national penal press journalism contest. The latter said in part: "There was some local criticism of my article that went something like, 'It's fine in theory but life doesn't work that way.' I plan to write an editorial, drawing from our current situation, our immediate predicament, showing that life does indeed work this way and I shall show them an exact circumstance from prison where, from the depths of despair and futility a man was able to mold for himself a meaningful and significant life experience. They, also, would not believe that a man under these circumstances could possibly undergo a transmutation which would turn despair into triumph. I shall attempt to show them that not only is this a possibility, it is a necessity."

Noös Cannot Become Sick

The concept of the noëtic dimension helps us understand and improve ourselves and helps the therapist understand and improve mental health. The therapist must try to reach this human dimension in patients because it contains the core of their humanity. According to logotherapy, sickness can originate in our *noös;* but unlike our body and psyche, the *noös,* our spirit, can never become sick. This is what Frankl calls his first, his psychiatric, credo: the belief that the noëtic person exists even behind the curtain of the symptoms of a psychotic illness. If this were not so, he points out, it would not be worth the physician's while to "repair" the psychophysical organism. If the doctor sees only the patient's organism and not also the noëtic person behind it, he or she becomes a medical mechanic and tacitly admits the patient is nothing but a human machine. The late psychoanalyst Franz Alexander warned physicians against developing a "plumber mentality," repairing patients as though they were faulty faucets.

The logotherapist elicits help from the patient's noëtic center, even if it is buried by a mountain of psychophysical symptoms. The defiant power of the human spirit is evoked to rebel against seemingly all-powerful forces of the psyche and the body. This is Frankl's second, his psychotherapeutic, credo: the belief that not only the noëtic part of the person remains well even if the surrounding psychophysical area has become sick but also that the noëtic self has the power to rise above the afflictions of the psychophysical self. Patients may not be able to change their condition, but they *can* change their attitude toward their own, perhaps incurably sick, psychophysical area.

On an American tour Frankl briefly met a woman who, because of incurable glandular trouble, weighed more than three hundred pounds. She was ashamed to go among people; she could not hold a job; her marriage had broken up. Psychiatric treatment had not helped. Frankl had no time for therapy, but he spent an hour talking to her. To her amazement he paid little attention to her affliction (once he realized the incurable situation) but stressed two points: that her condition was beyond her control and she would do best to take it as unchangeable and that she should give attention to all the things she still could do, even as an overweight woman. Although he never mentioned words like "noëtic," he succeeded in making her see that behind all that fat and those depressions triggered by her physical condition there was her true self, which still could live a full life, in spite of her bodily handicap. "One does not have to stand for every nonsense from oneself," Frankl told her and pointed out to her that she had already made a good beginning: other people in her place might have become alcoholics or committed suicide. He encouraged her to take her affliction as a challenge, to see the values life had to offer other than physical slimness, and perhaps to become an inspiration to other overweight women who, like herself, are trapped in a physical situation beyond their control.[3] A year later, when Frankl passed through her city on another tour, the woman came to thank him. "Your one talk did me more good than years of treatment," she told him. She felt calmer, more hopeful, had "rejoined the human race." And for the first time in years she had actually lost thirty pounds. Frankl later commented to the doctors at the hospital where the case had been presented to him that while her physical condition had remained incurable, existential relief had brought some small help even in that area.

The Noëtic Unconscious

A frequently raised question concerns the role of the unconscious in logotherapy. Implied is a suspicion that logotherapy pays little or no attention to the unconscious and thus disregards one of Freud's greatest contributions to the understanding of human nature. In reality the opposite is true. Both logophilosophy and logotherapy are strongly based on a concept of the human unconscious that not only accepts Freud's views but extends them.

Freud was a giant but, as Frankl comments in *The Doctor and the Soul* (p. 3), even "a dwarf standing on the shoulders of a giant can see farther than the giant himself." From Freud's shoulders Frankl sees in the unconscious not only the psychological and instinctual but also an area of the noëtic. From the shoulders of Carl Jung he sees in the noëtic unconscious not merely the collective and archetypal but something personal and existential. Frankl sees the noëtic part of the unconscious as a region in which we are not an ego driven by an id but a self, a person relating to others as human beings to be loved and understood rather than things to be used and manipulated.

In this noëtic realm of our unconscious we make our great existential decisions. From here we draw our artistic inspiration, our religious faith, our beliefs, and our intuitions. From this part of our unconscious comes the muffled voice of our conscience telling us our tasks and by so doing directing us to the meanings of our lives.

Freud's unconscious is a realm into which sexual desires and aggressiveness can be repressed, causing neuroses; Frankl sees another part of the unconscious, in which our will to meaning can be repressed, causing a feeling of inner emptiness, of meaninglessness, "the existential vacuum." One might say, perhaps with some oversimplification, that the instinctual unconscious contains much that is wrong with us (and that we do not want to face) and that our spiritual unconscious contains much of what is right with us (and that we have ignored). Frankl's distinction between the instinctual and the spiritual, in addition to Freud's distinction between the conscious and unconscious, can be schematized in the following manner:

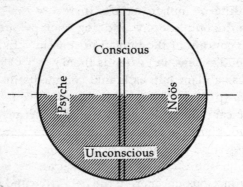

These theoretical concepts must, of course, not be visualized in any physical sense as horizontal and vertical dividers. The fundamental difference is this: The borderline between the conscious and the unconscious is fluid—psychoanalysis is based on the assumption that the conscious can be repressed into the unconscious and that the unconscious can be made conscious in analysis. But the line between psyche and *noös* is firm. "The line between the spiritual and the instinctual," Frankl states in *The Unconscious*

God (p. 26), "cannot be drawn sharply enough." The important distinction is not whether something is conscious or unconscious but rather whether it pertains to the id or to the self—whether it is rooted in our instincts and propels us or whether it emerges from our center and allows us to make our own decisions. Our scientific age has made conscious reason our king and ruler. In the first half of this century the king had to face the revolution of the unconscious—our repressed drives—and now, in the second half of this century, the revolution of the neglected human spirit.

The expansion of the unconscious beyond the instinctual to include the noëtic has important consequences for the diagnosis, cure, and prevention of sickness. Just as psychoanalysis assumes that drives and instincts that have been repressed and have caused neuroses must be made conscious to achieve healing, so logotherapy assumes that our will to meaning, when it has been repressed or thwarted and has caused a feeling of meaninglessness or existential frustration, must be made conscious so life will become meaningful. The methods logotherapy uses to achieve its goals are discussed in Chapter IX.

Meaning—An Existential Answer

To the logotherapist the human dimension is the key to our search for meaning and the spiritual unconscious, the major resource in this search. Unlike in Freud's time, our major problem no longer is the repression of our natural desire for pleasure, especially sexual pleasure. In our sexually liberated, affluent, science-oriented, skeptical, and fatalistic society we suffer from the repression of another natural desire—to find meaning. The repression of our will to meaning causes us to feel that life has no purpose, no challenge, no obligations; that it makes no difference what we do; that life is overpowering; that we have no more significance than an insect under a steam roller. We feel hopelessly trapped by circumstances beyond our control. We are "stuck," defeated by life. Life is a rat race, a treadmill, and there is a vast emptiness in us. The existential vacuum exists among rich and poor, young and old, the successes and the failures. As logotherapists could show, business executives try to fill it with extra work and students try to fill it with drugs. The existential vacuum lurks behind many feverish attempts to fill this emptiness—with sex, alcohol, defiance of authority, fast cars, committee work, television viewing, overeating, and even such respected activities as politics, psychoanalysis, and religion. The feeling of emptiness is especially widespread among the youth. Forty percent of Frankl's Austrian students and 81 percent of his American students confessed to it, and similar figures have been reported in other universities. The existential vacuum was prominent in a survey of one hundred prosperous Harvard alumni: one-fourth of them doubted that their lives had any meaning. The same doubt was reported as existing in the Communist countries by Czech journals of psychiatry.

The existential vacuum, however, is no disease. The frustration of our will to meaning does not bring on neurosis any more than a frustration of our will to pleasure automatically leads to sickness. On the contrary, the repression of sexual desire can be a great human achievement if it is done for the sake of a higher value—a man and a woman's respect and love for each other or a priest's respect and love for God. Frankl disagrees with Freud's statement that to doubt the meaning of life is a symptom of sickness. On the contrary, such doubts may trigger our search for meaning, and logotherapy uses our thirst for a meaningful existence to maintain or recover mental health.

People respond with relief when they are assured that their feeling of inner emptiness is by no means a symptom of mental disease but rather a challenge to fill this emptiness—a challenge to which only a human being can rise. At present, when so many people are psychological hypochondriacs, always looking for childhood traumas, rejections, and other psychological excuses for their failures and confusions, they find strength in the message that their feeling of meaninglessness is not a symptom of sickness but proof of their humanness. Only humans can feel the lack of meaning because only they are aware of meaning.

A New Type of Neurosis

There is, however, a danger. Into this existential vacuum mental disease may enter. Doubting the meaning of life may lead to despair, depression, and a new type of neurosis for which Frankl has coined a new term—"noögenic" neurosis. Noögenic neuroses do not originate in the patient's psyche and are not brought about by such traditional Freudian causes as repressed sexuality, childhood traumas, or conflicts between different drives or between the id, ego, and superego. Noögenic neuroses originate in our noëtic dimension and may be brought about by value collisions, by conflicts of conscience, or by the unrewarded groping for our highest value—an ultimate meaning of life. Psychologists at Harvard University and at Bradley Center, Columbus, Georgia, developed tests to distinguish between such noögenic neuroses and other, more conventional forms. The Georgia tests, using twelve hundred patients, consistently support Frankl's thesis that we are really dealing with a new syndrome.[4] In these cases, psychoanalysis' orthodox approach of going back to the past to search for causes hidden in the psyche will be of little avail. Noögenic neuroses respond to a therapy that draws the patient's awareness to the present and the future, to commitments to fulfill, relationships to establish, and meanings to uncover.

It is central to logotherapeutic belief that under normal circumstances we can solve clashes of conscience and value conflicts by ourselves and that the therapist's role is merely to help patients see they are *not* helpless victims of their upbringing, surroundings, and inner drives, that they can take a stand, as healthy persons will. It is, however, possible that value conflicts or "existential frustration" can overwhelm a person and lead to neurosis.

In our era of swift changes an increasing number of people are being caught between "old" and "new" values: the church-supported virtue of having many children versus the call to help prevent a potentially disastrous population expansion; the virtue of virginity versus the approval of one's peers; the value of making a career as an employee versus the value of independence; the value of a well-paying, though meaningless, job versus the value of following one's calling to become an artist; or the value of growing roots in a community versus that of a profitable career after a transfer out of town. It is significant that in recent years human conflicts often concern job security, salaries, and material goods versus such "old-fashioned" values as taking over the family business, excellence of workmanship, and rugged individualism. Psychiatrists have observed that even the anxieties of so-called endogenous depressions have changed during recent years. One generation ago many patients blamed themselves, feeling guilty before their conscience, their parents, their community, or God. As Frankl indicates in *Psychotherapy and Existentialism*, today's endogenously depressed patients are worried more about their health and their ability to earn money or to keep up their payments. They display anxieties connected with their jobs or getting old. Frankl once quipped that depressive patients nowadays are concerned less with Judgment Day and more with payday.

Logotherapy was developed to understand, diagnose, and

possibly cure noögenic neuroses. But, equally important, the concepts that led to the development of logotherapy help us take a new look at the human being—not only at the neurotic person but at all human beings with their struggles, ambitions, failures, triumphs, and lifelong pursuit of meaning.

3. What Is the Meaning of Life?

Only a life lived for others is worthwhile.

ALBERT EINSTEIN

The three tenets of logotherapy can be tested by experience and have been found acceptable by people regardless of belief—Jesuits and Orthodox Jews, atheists and agnostics. To repeat, the tenets are:

Life has meaning under all conditions.
We have the "will to meaning" and become happy only when we feel we are fulfilling our meaning.
We have the freedom, within obvious limitations, to fulfill the meaning of our lives.

Ultimate Meaning

As was indicated in the Introduction, meaning is seen on two levels: the ultimate meaning of life and the meaning of the moment. Ultimate meaning presupposes an order in which we as individuals have a part, even if it is infinitesimal. The order may be called God, life, nature, or—a term becoming widely acceptable—the ecosystem. God's order (the will, or word, of God, the traditional translation of *logos*) is not always clear to us mortals. The order of life, "what life is all about," has been interpreted differently by philosophers. The order of nature is more clearly defined through the sciences, at least in the field of the physical sciences. The ecosystem extends our awareness of order into the field of ethics: We see that violations of natural laws have consequences beyond the physical, we refrain from interrupting the chain of life and poisoning our natural resources because it is harmful for us and others, now and into the future. We are moral not because we are told to be but because we see the practical consequences of immorality. In the area of the ecosystem the "will of God" has become at least partly visible and demonstrable. We see that "sinning"—going against the order—carries its own punishment, that there are laws beyond human laws, and that we face demands we can refuse only at our own peril. We recognize a flow in life, to use an Eastern image, that we can follow, struggle against, or ignore. We know what Albert Einstein meant when he said he could not imagine God playing dice with the universe.

This grandiose order, I believe, is what Frankl understands by *logos*, ultimate meaning. We can never hope to "find" it in its totality, we can only pursue it to the best of our abilities. But neither can we "invent" it arbitrarily. Life, Frankl says, is not like a Rorschach test, a meaningless blotch into which we can read our meanings. He sees life more as a hidden-picture puzzle, one of those puzzles that shows many lines presenting clouds, trees, houses, and people with the caption asking us to find the bicycle. We have to turn the picture this way and that, and after patience and effort we may find the bicycle hidden in the confusion of lines. But in life we never can find the "bicycle" of meaning in the confusion of events. We may glimpse it in fleeting moments of peak experiences, but even then the ultimate answer escapes us because life poses always bigger and more complex puzzles. The pursuit of ultimate meaning requires a constant search in which it does make a difference what we decide to do and refuse to do.

His belief in an ultimate meaning has provoked the accusation that Frankl is "sneaking in religion by the back door." If "religion" means a belief in ultimate meaning located in a dimension beyond the human, then the accusation has substance. The definition of religion in this widest possible sense is precisely the definition offered by Albert Einstein when he said that having found an answer to the question of the meaning of life means to be religious. The conviction that there is something greater than human existence has been expressed in many ways, from Nietzsche's observation that man must overcome himself and strive toward superman, to Tillich's and Barth's insistence that man is not the ground of his being.

Clinical observations convinced Frankl that human existence always is directed toward meaning, however little we may be aware of it. In a German essay, Frankl wrote, "There exists something like a foreknowledge of a meaning; and a precognition of meaning is also the basis of what logotherapy calls 'the will to meaning.' Whether or not we want to, we do believe in meaning as long as we have a breath of air inside us. Even a person committing suicide believes in meaning—if not in continuing to live, then in dying. If he really no longer believed in any meaning at all, he could not move a finger, and thus could not commit suicide."[1]

Frankl's observations have been confirmed by Elisabeth Kübler-Ross's research on dying persons. Even atheists close to death radiate a strange calm and security that cannot be explained by their atheistic views but only by a trust in an ultimate meaning that goes beyond the rationalizations of their atheism.

The Meaning of the Moment

It may be disappointing to read about a philosophy that places meaning at its core and then goes on to say we can never fully find it but have to chase it like a will-o'-the-wisp. Fortunately, there is a meaning we can and indeed must find in order to lead a meaningful life. This is what might be called the "meaning of the moment." We are seen as unique individuals, going from birth to death through a string of unique life situations. Every situation, every unrepeatable moment, offers a specific meaning potential. To respond to these meaning offerings of the moment is to lead a meaningful life.

The meaning of the moment differs from moment to moment and from person to person. For instance, at this particular moment we are joined in one and the same situation: I speak to you through my book, and you "hear" what I say. Yet the meanings of the moment are different. For me it is to explain logotherapy. For you, if the meaning of the moment is indeed in reading this book, the meanings will be varied. For one reader it may be intellectual curiosity; she may want to learn something. For a second reader the meaning may be a hope that the book will help with a personal problem. For a third it may be the hope of finding something to help another person he cares about. For a fourth it may be professional ambition: to find something he can use as a counselor, teacher, or social worker. For a fifth the meaning of the moment could be to fulfill a school assignment. For a sixth it may be to read to a blind person. For a seventh it may be just a book to help her fall asleep. Whatever the meaning of the moment is for you right now, it will not necessarily remain so in the future. Many readers have told me that when they reread my book, many previously marked passages had become irrelevant and others passed over had attained new meaning for them.

When you lay down this book, you enter new situations with new meaning potentials: to go to class, cook dinner, go on a date, or sleep. Most meanings of the moment are trivial and most decisions are made in our unconscious. Each decision has consequences, and some are far-reaching, although we do not always realize it. Some moments require tremendous decisions; the demands seem overwhelming and all our spiritual resources are required to respond to them. Every one of those hundred thousand moments of which our lives consist contains a specific meaning for us, and for us alone. It is our task to find the unique meaning of each moment. It is an awesome and glorious task, but we have two helpers to accomplish it: our conscience and our values. They are discussed in later chapters.

The Demand Quality of Meaning

Both ultimate meaning and the meanings of the moment place demands upon us. Logotherapy sees us as always reaching out, pursuing goals. Human existence, Frankl maintains, always points at something beyond itself . . . a meaning to fulfill or another human being to encounter lovingly (*PE*, p. 90). This call to find meaning in self-transcendence has long been a religious demand, often tied to specific creeds or dogmas. The "nonbeliever" (in a specific approach to truth) was condemned to the hell of meaninglessness. But psychiatry, as a branch of medicine, cannot restrict its healing methods to the religious, even less to the sectarian. Frankl stresses that the psychiatrist is obliged, if by nothing else than professional ethics, to help all patients alike. If health depends on meaning, then the nonreligious patient has as much right to expect help as the religious. The religious therapist has no right to lead the atheistic patient onto a religious path to find meaning; the atheistic therapist has no right to discourage the religious patient from finding meaning within his or her particular faith. Patients must be allowed to discover meanings in their frame of reference, be it religious orthodoxy or liberalism, humanism or atheism. What matters is that they become aware that they are free to find meaning, have the responsibility to do so, and that no one can do it for them. The pursuit of the unique meanings of our life makes us a unique personality—a chosen person, as it were—not because we belong to a certain religion or sect but because we are a human being.

In this connection Frankl quotes a famous passage by Hillel, a contemporary of Jesus: "If I don't do it, who will do it? If I don't do it now, when shall I do it? And if I do it for myself, what am I" (*WH*, p. 55)? He sees in these three questions the essence of logotherapy. The first part says, "I am irreplaceable." The second says, "Each moment is unrepeatable." And the third says that if I do it only for my sake, I am not true to my human nature.

Two thousand years later the same idea was expressed by Shlomo Bardin, director of the Brandeis Institute in California, who called us "the trustees of life." We are responsible to carry out as best we can what is entrusted to us, to develop our potentials, make the best of our life, to use it as a great opportunity. The German poet Friedrich Hebbel put it this way: "Life is not anything; it is only the opportunity for something."[2]

To Frankl, our will to meaning—though unconscious and often explained away by ideologies concerned with psychophysical phenomena—is our primary motivation. In a seminar a student challenged Frankl's concept that our will to meaning was more basic than our will to pleasure. The newborn baby, the student argued, obviously has a will to pleasure but no will to meaning. This argument, Frankl replied, is as valid as saying that crying is more basically human than speaking because babies show a great capacity for crying before they can speak. He concluded that something may be basically human and yet manifest itself only in later stages of development.

Demands for meaning often came from religious and secular values in the past. Our values, however, as discussed in the next chapter, are changing as the knowledge of our world expands rapidly. The world in which we shall die is not the same one into which we were born. Our parents' generation, born in the horse-and-buggy age, lived long enough to die in the jet age. Our own generation, born in the Model-T age, will die in the satellite age or beyond. Our children can no more imagine what life in the pre-Freudian era was like than we can imagine what it was like to live in the times before Newton. Even our method of acquiring new knowledge has undergone a basic change. In an age of science we are prone to accept truths not by faith but by scrutiny. We are less likely to accept what Bishop Pike called the "prefab truth" that comes from sacred books and sages of the past. We are looking for truths that can be researched in repeatable experiments. What this does to religion, which is based on unrepeatable personal experiences, we are only beginning to understand. The impact of scientific thinking makes us disregard phenomena that cannot be measured but are subject to judgment and faith. At first glance this seems to destroy religion, but in the long run religion will be strengthened because it is being placed on foundations accepted not only in the dark shrines of the churches but also in the bright laboratories.

Today the inspired searchers of old, the prophets, sages, and artists, are joined by scientists to provide contemporary answers to ancient questions. Logotherapy is based on the assumption that even in our era of doubt and nonfaith we must find a firm foundation to understand our existence, to acquire the courage to decide about our actions, and to realize that this foundation can only be found when valid ancient truths are combined with current views of the physical sciences, existential philosophy, and psychiatry.

Pragmatic Approach

The search for meaning starts on a simple, day-by-day level by responding to the situation of the moment, by accepting the simple tasks of life. Frankl illustrated this point to me when I first interviewed him at the Poliklinik Hospital in Vienna: "The meaning of the situation for you is to ask questions; for me, to answer them; for my nurse, to keep visitors away and answer the phone so we can talk undisturbed. And an hour from now the meaning of the moment might be for me to see a patient, for you to go sightseeing in Vienna, and for my nurse to make appointments for patients."

This pragmatic approach to the problem of meaning was discussed at a seminar I conducted for scientists in the San Francisco area. One chemist pointed out that Frankl's way was the way of science. "He states the hypothesis that life has meaning. Then he encourages the patient to take a lamp and step into the dark. He will see only a very limited circle of light around him. Then Frankl suggests that the patient hold his lamp higher and take further steps, one at a time, as his surroundings become visible. In this manner, eventually, he may find his path."

This is the task of the logotherapist: to illuminate, to let meaning "shine forth." But behind the simple meanings of the moment lie larger tasks. In our Vienna interview, for instance, beyond the immediate tasks of the situation were the larger tasks: for Frankl, to spread the message of logotherapy; for me, to gather material for my book; for the nurse, to help the doctor. Still further lie even more universal tasks: to speak to the needs and cure the ills of our age, to be a truthful reporter, to be a conscientious nurse. One has to start with the first step: One cannot be a great physician without paying careful attention to the specific moment and to the individual patient at hand. Frankl, an enthusiastic Alpinist, compares the step-by-step approach in the world of meaning finding with a basic rule of rock climbing: On the steepest precipice do not worry about the abyss below or about the difficulties ahead. Concentrate on the immediate task—the next firm grip, the next toehold.

Meaningful Activities

Although Frankl warns against "prescribing" meanings, he helps patients see three areas where they can find meaning: creative activities (work, hobbies, or devotion to a task), experiences (encounters with works of art, nature, or other human beings) and attitudes (when, in a hopeless situation, we make use of that inner freedom no one can ever take from us—the freedom to take a stand against an unalterable fate).

Today it becomes increasingly difficult to find meaning in work. Fewer and fewer jobs provide meaningful activities; they do not challenge us as a human being but only provide an opportunity to function (and not very efficiently) as part of a machine. Meaning-fulfilling work still exists—for research scientists, physicians, policy-making executives, ministers, and creative artists, for instance. Yet holders of routine jobs, too—factory workers, clerks, sales representatives, computer operators, may see relevance in their work. A patient once complained to Frankl: "It's easy for you, professor, you are a psychiatrist, you can find meaning in your work. But what can I find in mine, as a carpenter?" Frankl's answer was that carpenters who fulfill their task to the limits of their capabilities can find as much meaning as physicians who fulfill their job the best they can and that the efforts of a clerk can be as meaningful as those of an artist. What matters is not the kind of work but the motivation. The artist whose main goal is to make money with work that remains below his or her best talents will find less meaning than the sales representative who sells a needed item at a fair price. "What matters," Frankl told the carpenter, "is not how large the radius of your activities is, but how well you fill its circle."[3]

But even with the best intention it sometimes is difficult

to find meaning in one's particular work. Fortunately, with working hours becoming shorter we have more opportunity to find meaningful activities during leisure hours through adult education courses, volunteer work for hospitals, community or neighborhood improvement, precinct work for a political party, or artistic pursuits. However, to be meaningful such activities have to be the kind that will fill the existential vacuum rather than help us run away from it.

Changing jobs is not always the solution. It may create rather than solve noögenic conflicts in the jobholders and members of their families. Such conflicts can be brought about by some companies' policy of moving their executives up the ladder by moving them around the country and even abroad. The male sales manager of an automobile company who was transferred every few years to a different area suffered a nervous breakdown whose noögenic origin was illuminated by a recurring dream in which he saw himself as a car that was turned in annually for a new model. An engineer's wife suffered from depression when her husband was made supervisor and transferred to a small company town where she had no friends at the time her children left home to marry and go to college. The seven-year-old daughter of an oil company executive began to stutter after her mother had been promoted three times in two years, each time moving to a different city.

But job conflicts are not restricted to the executive level. Any job may cause a clash between material and human values. We may have taken on work that was satisfying in youth but is no longer challenging. Then we must decide whether to find new ways to fill the circle of our present situation or to make a break for something new with higher challenges. Value clashes often come to light in my sharing groups. A thirty-five-year-old ex-toolmaker said, "I hate that eighteen-year-old boy who decided that I should become a toolmaker. Not that I was a failure. I made a lot of money, and if I had been married and had children, I probably would have remained a toolmaker for the sake of my family. But I felt that I was meant to be a teacher, so I quit my job and went back to college." A forty-two-year-old biochemist, married and mother of three, gave up the tenure of a full professorship, went to divinity school to become a minister, and later insisted on taking a church in a slum area. A composer gave up a $50,000-a-year job in Hollywood and went to live in the Big Sur area with his wife and four children, writing folksongs on subjects he feels are important, such as ecology and peace. He refuses to make commercial use of these compositions. "If you want to hear my songs," this twentieth-century troubadour tells people, "you have to invite me to your living room or to your church." A minister who felt her true beliefs no longer conformed to what was expected of her by her denomination and by the elders of her church accepted a minor position in a more liberal denomination. These examples from contemporary California illustrate the fact that we can choose new, meaningful commitments.

The Meaning of Personal Experience

The second area in which, according to logotherapy, we can find meaning is that of experiencing beauty, truth, or love. If we are listening to a perfect performance of a favorite symphony and someone asks whether life has meaning, there can be no doubt about our answer. The same is true for a nature lover on a mountain, a religious person at a memorable service, an intellectual at an inspiring lecture, an artist in front of a masterpiece, or a scientist at the moment of discovery.

Those are peak experiences. "One moment," Frankl maintains, "can retroactively flood an entire life with meaning."[4] He remembers the "spiritual shivers" when, at the age of sixteen, he read Freud's *Beyond the Pleasure Principle*. This was an experience of truth discovered. He also recalls what it meant to him suddenly to see the sunset through the barbed wire in the concentration camp—an experience of beauty. But the greatest experience is that of mature love—to know one human being in his or her uniqueness.

Love means that someone steps up to us, selecting us among the four billion people on earth and saying, "You, and no one else." Love is logotherapy in full action. The lover not only sees the present "thou" in us, but also the multitude of potentials open to us—potentials we may not be aware of. "In love the self is not driven by the id, but rather the self chooses the Thou" (*UG*, p. 37). In love, we "see in the partner another person . . . in his [or her] uniqueness" (*UC*, p. 81), and we not only say "yes," to our partner as he or she is at the present, but see future potentials which we help to develop.

I arrived in New York a penniless refugee, jobless at the tail end of the depression, an ex-attorney with knowledge of laws no longer existing even in my own country, a writer without a language. I met a woman who did not care what I had (or did not have) and who perceived what I was—what I could become if only someone believed in me. She did not tell me this; she acted upon it by marrying me.

The Meaning of Attitudes

Meanings in activities and experiences are easily perceived. More difficult to see is Frankl's contention that meaning can also be found in attitudes when we face unavoidable suffering. There is no need to seek suffering as a source of meaning; that would be meaningless masochism. But when we face what Frankl calls "the tragic triad" (*PE*, p. 56)—unavoidable suffering, inerasable guilt, and death—we still have the possibility "to transform suffering into a heroic and victorious achievement" (*PE*, p. 83), to use Frankl's phrase, and to bear witness to what a human being still is capable of, even in defeat.

The deaths of Jesus and Socrates have been inspirations for centuries, giving testimony to what a human being can do for the sake of love or truth. Even ordinary men and women can become heroes if they see meaning in their actions, as did the British during the air attacks of World War II and the Berliners during the air lift. They were aware, even if unconsciously, of a meaning behind their suffering and of the example they set for the rest of the world.

A story is told about Tristan Bernard, the French writer who with his wife was taken to the Drancy concentration camp by the Nazis. While they were marching in a column of despairing Jews, Bernard said to his wife, "Up to now we have lived in fear; from now on we will live in hope." From the depth of a situation of despair he had reversed their outlook, not by changing the situation but by changing his attitude. His example helped his fellow sufferers face life with new courage.

Every country has stories of heroes who found meaning in dying for a cause they believed in. Their examples live on. Examples also shine forth from unsung heroes. A young man told me how his grandfather died. "There he lay, in a miserable nursing home. We never had thought much of him; he was considered an oddball, a 'moocher.' But when we visited him, it was he who cheered us up. He gave us children a priceless gift: he showed us how to die with dignity. We had to reevaluate our opinions about him. Thanks to him, death has lost its terror."

No birth is without labor pains, figuratively and literally. The history of creative people is full of tales of pain, from Michelangelo's "agony and ecstasy" to Handel's complete physical exhaustion upon giving birth to his *Messiah*. It is also questionable whether the moments of bliss in a love relationship could be possible without the "labor pains" of agony and doubt. Yet no true artists would forego their creations, or lovers their love, because pain is the price. And neither would a mother forego her child because she knows she will have to endure what is probably the most universal human "suffering" in the world. On the contrary, she is happily suffering pain for the sake of having a child. Imagine, however, her anguish were she to know in advance that her baby was going to be incurably retarded. Yet, when in some unfortunate cases parents are faced with this unavoidable fact, many have turned this suffering into an achievement by devoting their love to the child, setting an example to other parents in similar tragic circumstances. It is not the load that breaks us down, logotherapy seems to say, but the way we carry it.

How Logotherapy Deals with Suffering

"There is no condition that cannot be ennobled either by a deed or by suffering." With these words the German poet Goethe anticipated the basic idea of logotherapy by more than a century. Logotherapy cannot prevent unavoidable suffering; it can keep people from despair. By Frankl's definition despair is caused by suffering in which the sufferer sees no meaning. Suffering in itself has no meaning, but we can assume meaningful attitudes toward events that in themselves are meaningless.

Ms. K. was in despair because she was going blind. With the help of another woman who had been born blind she learned Braille and became so interested in the method that she volunteered to transcribe books in Braille script. Her work brought her into contact with other blind people and they formed book discussion groups for the blind. By the time she lost her eyesight entirely her life was so full she had no time to worry.

This example illustrates the most hopeful aspect of finding meaning by a change of attitude: it is exactly in the area of the despair that the patient can find help. As Alcoholics Anonymous has shown, alcoholics can find meanings through their very problem because no one can help an alcoholic better than one who knows the situation from experience. The best help for a woman in despair because her husband left her comes from another woman who can say to her: "Yes, I know how you feel because I went through the same thing five years ago. I was so low I thought of killing myself. But looking back to that time I see that a lot of good has come from my period of suffering. I realized that I can be independent; I developed skills I never dreamed I had; I made new friends. Just wait and see."

Patience is sometimes necessary in order to see meaning behind suffering. But patience is not always possible, for instance with people facing death. A man in the cancer ward of the Stanford University Hospital who had been told he had only three months to live said "If you think I will sit here for three months waiting to die you have another think coming." Every day, as long as he had the strength, he made the rounds among other cancer patients, talking to them about their feelings regarding this shared fate. One of the doctors in the ward commented: "No one can do this as well as a person they know is dying, too. Not even the doctor. What does the doctor know about dying? He is not the one facing death." The meanings patients can find in unavoidable suffering must be found on the patient's, not the doctor's, terms. Nonreligious persons will discover meanings in a variety of ways—for the sake of a child, a friend, their country, a scientific discovery, or to inspire others.

Religious persons, too, can find meaning behind suffering in a variety of ways, and it is an oversimplification to say they will find it for the sake of God. Here also the doctor must allow patients to find meaning on their own terms.

This is illustrated in the case of an orthodox rabbi who had lost his wife and six children in the concentration camp at Auschwitz. He had married again and was in deep despair because his second wife was sterile, thus he could not have a son to say the traditional Jewish prayers after his death. Frankl, trying to kindle hope in the patient, asked him if he did not expect to see his children in heaven, according to the patient's religious convictions. The question resulted in an outburst of tears. Now the true reason for the despair came to the fore: His children had died as innocent martyrs for the glory of God and thus would be found worthy of the highest place in heaven. He, however, as an old sinful man, could not expect to be assigned to the same place. This remark gave Frankl the chance to suggest the possibility that this might have been precisely the meaning of his survival. It might be an opportunity to be purified from sins by the years of suffering the children's loss so he, too, although not innocent as his children, might become worthy of joining them in heaven. Was it not written in the Psalms that God preserved all our tears? For the first time the rabbi saw the possibility of meaning behind his sufferings in his own religious terms. He left with a glimmer of hope that his suffering might not have been in vain after all.

How logotherapy can deal with unavoidable suffering is also illustrated by the case of Sister Michaela of the rigid Order of the Carmelites. She suffered from severe depressions and had considered suicide. She particularly suffered from guilt based on her belief that as a good Christian her faith should be strong enough to conquer her sickness. Frankl diagnosed her condition as "endogenous" depression and prescribed appropriate drugs. But he also stressed that her depression had a primarily organic cause; hence she was not responsible for it. Thus the fact that she suffered from the depression was not due to any failure on her part, but how she took it could constitute a mental and spiritual achievement. After a few therapeutic sessions the patient was relaxed and in better spirits. She remarked, "I am at peace with myself and grateful. I have accepted this cross." She later showed Frankl an entry in her diary, which he treasures as a testimony to the defiant power of the human spirit. It reads in part:

> I am exposed to unknown forces which overwhelm my will— quite helplessly exposed am I. Sadness is my steady companion; whatever I do, it weighs me down like lead upon my soul. Where are my ideals? Gone—as all the good and beautiful things for which I used to strive. Nothing but yawning boredom fills my heart. I live as if thrown into a vacuum, and at times not even pain is accessible to me. In this distress I call God, the Father of all, and even God is silent. I wish for only one thing—to die. If I had not the faithful awareness that I am not the master over my life, I would have ended it many times; but through this awareness the bitterness of my sufferings is suddenly transmuted. For, a person who assumes that his life must consist of stepping from success to success is like a fool who stands next to a building site and shakes his head because he cannot understand why people dig deep down when they set out to build a cathedral. God builds a temple out of each man's soul, and in my case he is just starting out to excavate the foundations. It is my task to offer myself to His excavations [WM, p. 132].

In emphasizing the meaning potential of suffering, Frankl runs contrary to the current tendency of U.S. society, which is so success- and happiness-centered that people are apt to hide their suffering as if it were shameful. Suffering as a possible source of achievement is likely to be rejected by a nation that automatically answers the question "How are you?" with a smile and "I'm fine," regardless. When Frankl lectured the first time to an American scientific society, he spoke of the meaning that can be elicited in people when they face suffering and death bravely and with dignity and felt his audience rejected his idea. After the lecture one of the leading Horney psychiatrists told him, "Dr.

Frankl, don't be surprised that they fight you—they envy you because you have suffered and they have not." He later was told the same thing when he lectured at Harvard. But since then some American psychiatrists have spoken up in support of Frankl's positive attitude toward the unavoidable fact of human suffering. Edith Weisskopf-Joelson of the University of Georgia has pointed out that Frankl's value system "may help counteract certain trends in our present-day civilization, where the incurable sufferer is given little opportunity to be proud of his unavoidable and incurable suffering, and to consider it ennobling rather than degrading."[5]

Perhaps the meaning of suffering cannot be understood by logic alone; it has to be experienced. Frankl's favorite statement comes from Yehuda Bacon, who as a boy survived the Auschwitz death camp and is now an artist in Israel. When he was liberated from the camp, it had been his ambition to tell everyone what had happened so it would not happen again and thus make the world a better place. He soon discovered that people did not want to know. He realized that as far as improving humanity was concerned his suffering had been in vain. But he found meaning in another area. "Suffering can have a meaning," he said, "if it changes *you* [the sufferer] for the better" (*WM*, p. 79).

Our Response to Meaning

Some theaters use a transparent screen for special effects. If a landscape or the interior of a room is projected on the screen, it can serve as a backdrop for the scene played before it. If the stage behind the screen is lit up, however, the screen becomes invisible and only the stage behind can be seen. The screen is a useful image to understand how we see meaning in life. French existentialists such as Sartre and Camus see meaning as our projection on the empty screen of life. "Life has no meaning," they seem to say, "but we need meaning. Therefore we have to make our own meanings." They use phrases like "Man invents himself" or "Man projects himself." Logotherapy conceives meaning as hidden behind a screen, and we have to turn on the light to see it. We have to elucidate meaning. We cannot fabricate it arbitrarily or "will" it in the sense that we can say, "Enough of this meaningless life! From now on I will have meaning." Nor can we will love in a general way; it comes in response to someone or something that has "turned on" the switch.

Another way to understand the concept of meaning is to see ultimate meaning as a supertransmitter, a *logos* in the center of the universe sending out meaning signals all the time in all directions. We all have our own little receiver in our conscience, still primitive and unreliable, trying to tune in on those broadcasts, trying to pick up signals.

Frankl uses a different image to explain how we see through our subjective perspective to perceive the objective reality behind it. We look at the world, he says, not as through a kaleidoscope but as through a telescope. In a kaleidoscope we see only what other human beings have put in, and the pattern depends on how we turn the kaleidoscope. But when we look through the telescope, we look beyond our subjective perspective. We look through it and at an objective world. And this is exactly the meaning of "perspective"—*perspicere* means to "look through." Although we all look from a different, subjective viewpoint, what we see is the same, the objective reality. Frankl presented this idea at the Harvard University Summer School in 1961. He pointed through the window at the Harvard Chapel outside and told his students: "That chapel out there presents itself from a different perspective to each of you depending on where you sit. If two of you were to claim that you see the chapel in exactly the same way, I would have to tell you that one of you is imagining things. But despite this different and highly subjective perspective, no one will deny that the Harvard Chapel out there is one and the same objective reality."[6]

The same is true when we look at a situation. We may differ in our interpretation of the meaning inherent in a situation, and not every interpretation is equally valid. To Frankl, finding the true meaning in a situation is like finding the right answer in a multiple-choice quiz. Several answers are possible; only one is right. Several interpretations of a situation are possible; only one is the true one.

In the winter 1966 issue of the *Journal of Existentialism* Frankl tells the following episode that illustrates the point. One evening in the question-and-answer period after a lecture the moderator helped sort out the questions handed in. He eliminated one as "sheer nonsense." He read the question as, "Dr. Frankl, how do you define 600 in your theory?" The question was written in block print; and when Frankl looked at it, he saw that it read, "Dr. Frankl, how do you define GOD in your theory?" Frankl considered this episode an unintentional projective test, all the more remarkable because the moderator, a theologian, had read "600" while Frankl, a neurologist, had read "GOD." The right interpretation was, of course, the one that understood the question the way the questioner meant it. That is why Frankl offers as a definition: "Meaning is what is meant."

Meant by what? By whom? Who poses life's questions? Society? Lawgivers? Conventions and traditions? God? Life itself? People will give many different answers. In any case it is something outside us, beyond us, that is doing the asking. It really matters little what name we give the questioner, just as it was of no consequence to know who had handed in the slip of paper. What does matter is to realize that questions require our response. The logotherapist's task is to make patients realize they are free to respond to the best of their abilities. In no case must therapists find the answer for the patients; they must not take the response-ability away from them but help them discover their own answers.

4. The Value of Values

> If men cannot always make history have a meaning, they can always act so that their own lives have one.
>
> ALBERT CAMUS

Frankl has developed the distinction between meaning and value only gradually. In his early writings he used the two terms together, often as synonyms; but where he applied them separately, value was the broader concept. In recent years the distinction has become clear: Meaning is "what is meant," he says, meant for you, in your present situation. It is specific, unique, and personal. You cannot take someone else's meaning or recover the meaning of a situation once it is past. Life and its string of meanings keeps rolling along. That is the basis for the logotherapeutic tenet that each person is unique—we live our unique life, have our unique opportunities, potentials, and shortcomings. We create unique relationships and accept unique tasks, face unique sufferings, experience unique guilt feelings, and die a unique death. The search for meaning is highly personal and distinct. But millions of people have gone through situations that were similar enough so they could react in a similar way. They found what was meaningful in standard situations. They found universal meanings, which is the way Frankl defines values: "meaning universals."

Help from Universal Values

The difference between "unique meanings" and "universal values" is illustrated by an incident in our sharing group. Ms. P. came to the meeting disturbed because a casual acquaintance, a woman in her fifties, had committed suicide the day before. Ms. P. had seen the woman just before she killed herself and said she seemed depressed and talked about her daughter's leaving home to accept a job in Denver. "If I had shown some interest," Ms. P. reproached herself, "perhaps taken her along to the church party to which I was going, I might have prevented the suicide. This was the task required of me at that moment, but I did not recognize it." In the discussion that followed others recalled similar instances. An elderly man told how years ago he had observed a neighbor's son shoplifting in a store but had said nothing because he did not want to get involved. The boy later went to prison for a holdup and our group member never forgave himself for having missed the opportunity of talking to the boy's father or the boy himself. Another participant, a man in his forties, sadly said, "When I was a kid I always avoided hugging and kissing my mother. I wish I could do it now but she's dead."

In those instances the unique meaning of a situation had been missed and was lost. Yet in each case that meaning could have been found with the help of values, those time-tested rules of behavior. Ms. P. might have been more attentive to the distressed woman by heeding the old advice to "love thy neighbor." The elderly man might have accepted his responsibility to speak to the boy's father by acting on his belief in the old virtue of honesty. The son of the unhugged mother might have followed the commandment, "Honor thy father and thy mother." It is true that such guidelines, rules, and commandments were developed for humankind as a whole, but under normal circumstances individuals benefit from them. They help decision making in confrontations with everyday life situations. If a man feels a sudden desire for his neighbor's wife, up springs a little warning light, "Thou shalt not covet . . ."; and the warning light is enforced by the law of the land, the power of the church, and the pressure of society. Universal values may even spare us decision making altogether: We simply follow generally accepted values. "Lovelorn column" choices are not based on the individual case (of which the columnist knows only one letter's worth) but on the wisdom of the ages—honesty is the best policy, be kind to people, mind your own business, and follow etiquette and ground rules. Occasionally, a new wisdom creeps into the columns, the not yet thoroughly tested wisdom of the twentieth century: If you are a woman, do not stand for any nonsense from your husband; and if you differ too much from the norm, see a psychiatrist.

Value Conflicts

Following general values rather than finding the unique meaning of a situation simplifies life but may prove costly, resulting in a conflict between two sets of overlapping or contradicting values. Such conflicts may even lead to neuroses. As Frankl expressed it graphically, specific meanings— being unique for each person and each situation—cannot overlap; they are nondimensional points along a line. (See illustration below.)

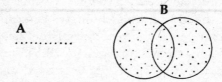

Each dot represents one unique meaning.

A illustrates the string of specific meanings of a person going through life, moment by moment. The meanings cannot overlap and cause conflicts.

In B, however, each circle represents the universal meanings (values) based on the meaning experiences of many people. Values help us make meaning decisions but may overlap, contradict each other, and cause conflicts, even neuroses.

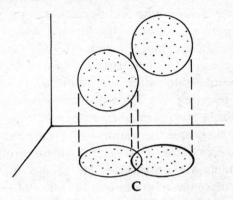

C

As shown in C, however, the overlapping takes place only when we remain in the physio-psychological plane. When we rise into the dimension of the human spirit, the values do not overlap but are ranked higher and lower. That means values do not overlap when we consider the human being in his or her three-dimensional totality. It also means that, while following values saves us the trouble of having to choose among meanings, we still have to make choices: we must assign priority to our values.

(Illustration adapted from Viktor E. Frankl, *The Will to Meaning,* [New York: New American Library, 1970], pp. 56, 57.)

Points cannot overlap. Values, however, are areas of universal meanings, covering many points of individual decisions, and may overlap. Overlapping values may cause the conflict of the conscientious objector torn between the value of his religious pacifistic upbringing and that of patriotism—love of country and of a society that values such feelings. Overlapping values may cause conflict for the young woman whose father wants her to take over the family business but who feels a commitment to the arts. Conflicts may develop for an executive caught between the values of career and family; for a politician caught between party loyalty and honesty; for a child having to choose between the values of two parents. Value conflicts sometimes break into the open when the overriding reality of some commitment is relaxed. A woman who had devoted years to her training for an executive position in the firm for which she worked became depressed when she reached her goal. A man who for years longed to be retired so he could "go fishing," found life unbearable after a few months of retirement. Often, after reaching our value goals, we are faced with the task of finding our personal meanings. If these are not pursued, emptiness and frustration—even despair—may result.

Frankl never ceases to stress that noëtic conflicts or spiritual problems are no disease. He relates the case of an American diplomat who came to his office after having undergone psychoanalysis for five years. The patient was dissatisfied with his career and found it difficult to implement the American foreign policy at that time. His analyst had told him to reconcile himself with his father because the American government, as well as his superiors, represented to him father images. Therefore his dissatisfaction with his job and the American foreign policy was caused by unconscious hatred of his father. The patient accepted the analyst's interpretation until, as Frankl expressed it, "he finally was unable to see the forest of reality because of the trees of symbols and images." After two interviews it became clear that the patient's will to meaning was frustrated in his career. He was longing for some other kind of work. There was no reason for the "patient" *not* to switch careers. When he did, his neurotic symptoms disappeared. "I doubt," Frankl commented, "that this man had any neurosis at all. He needed no psychotherapy, not even logotherapy. Not every conflict *per se*—and that is the lesson of the case—is necessarily neurotic."[1] Because value conflicts are no disease, logotherapy does not attempt to avoid them. Indeed, conflicts cannot be avoided. Like the search for meaning, they are specifically human phenomena and must be taken as part of human existence. Obviously, no one can live without value conflicts because practically everything in our lives causes conflicts—our upbringing, relationships to parents and friends, education, religion, society, work, marriage, even therapy. The New Zealand pediatrician, Margaret Liley, states in *The Infant World*, "There is no such thing as a completely untraumatic upbringing." Only in special circumstances will value conflicts lead to noögenic neuroses. For these cases logotherapy helps patients become fully conscious of their conflicts so they themselves can make decisions.

The following case illustrates a noögenic neurosis and logotherapy's approach to a cure. Ms. B., a young woman, came to the therapist because she was suffering from a severe neurosis and reactive depression.[2] It turned out her sickness was rooted in a conflict between the values of her religion and her marital vows. According to her upbringing, her children's religious education was of utmost importance to her; her atheistic husband was opposed to it. The conflict originated in her noëtic dimension but caused symptoms on the psychosomatic plane. To treat the symptoms—that is, the consequences of the ethical conflict—the psychiatrist prescribed the proper drugs. Then a therapy was begun that concerned itself with the *causes* of her neurosis. This was not possible unless questions of meanings and values were discussed. Ms. B. said she could lead a pleasant life and achieve peace of mind if she would adjust to the values of her husband and his peers. Her problem was to decide whether she should adjust to these values at the price of giving up her own. This was precisely what she found impossible to do. Adjusting to her husband's philosophy of life, she said, would mean "to sacrifice my own self." She stated, "To renounce my religious convictions would mean a surrender of my self." This remark was crucial. Had she not made it, the therapist could not have advised her. He could neither have encouraged her to adjust to her husband's atheism nor strengthened the patient's insistence on her religious beliefs. But now that she had expressed her commitment to religious values, the therapist explained to her that her neurosis was the result of an attempt to repress her spiritual aspirations and that, consequently, her neurosis could not be cured without her being true to herself. Ms. B. realized that she need not surrender her religious principles to those of her husband but that, for the sake of maintaining these religious principles, any provocation of her husband should be avoided while she gave him opportunities to understand her religious convictions better. The therapist helped Ms. B. regain her self-confidence, and this in turn became instrumental in her ability to persuade her husband to agree to a religious education for their children. As time went on, her religious convictions deepened, but not in the sense of institutionalized religiosity. She could face her husband's views and also what she regarded as the superficiality of his peer values with self-assurance and tolerance.

Hierarchy of Values

During the years Frankl refined his theory of values, he came to doubt his assumption that value conflicts are unavoidable. In "What is Meant by Learning" he proposes that values only *seem* to overlap and conflict when the noëtic dimension is disregarded. If we visualize values as spheres in three-dimensional space, they may not collide although their projections onto the two-dimensional plane do overlap. (See illustration.) Frankl sees value collisions as the result of neglecting the dimension in which there is room for a "higher" and a "lower," that is, a dimension where values have a hierarchy. This would mean that even in following values we are not spared decision making. Instead of deciding on the meaning of the moment, we have to decide which value we consider higher in our hierarchy of values. In practical therapy this means that patients who suffer from problems caused by value conflicts must be helped to decide their own hierarchy of values. This was the therapy undertaken with Ms. B.

Many problems caused by value conflicts can be solved without the help of a therapist. Frankl himself was faced dramatically with a value conflict when he and his first wife arrived in the Auschwitz concentration camp and the time came to say good-bye. When they were about to separate, he told her with great emphasis, so she would understand his meaning, "Stay alive at all costs. Go to any length to survive." He had become aware that in this unique situation it was his responsibility to give her his absolution in advance for whatever she might find necessary to preserve her life. She was a beautiful woman and it was possible that an SS officer would become interested in her. This could be her chance to save her life, but she might feel inhibited by the thought of her husband and the marital vows she had taken. Her upbringing had been strictly religious, along traditional lines, and Frankl knew that the value of marital fidelity was deeply rooted in her. He realized that a value conflict was threatening between two values, both based on the oldest rules of Western civilization—the Ten Commandments. One was the commandment not to commit adultery, the other, not to kill. For Frankl felt that by not releasing his wife from her moral obligations toward him he might have become co-responsible for her death. He might have indirectly contributed to her being killed, as he expressed it later, "for the sake of a husband's narcissism, if I had placed the commandment not to commit adultery above the one not to kill." A theologian, he conceded, might evade the dilemma by asserting that there is a hierarchy even within the Ten Commandments. "The commandments have been numbered from one to ten, but this numerical order does not imply a ranking of values. Each individual must find the rank of the commandments as the specific situation demands it. What I did in Auschwitz," he said, "was to make a decision in this specific situation whereby I gave second place to the (by us) generally highly regarded value of fidelity, in favor of a value which I felt the unique situation demanded: to give 'absolution' to my wife to anything she might have to do to save her life. This, I felt, was the requirement of the moment—a requirement, to be sure, that might have been valid neither before nor after this situation. For I do hope that saying goodbye in Auschwitz is a situation that will not occur again."[3]

We are constantly confronted with apparent value conflicts. We are constantly required to make value judgments, decisions between seemingly conflicting values, and decisions about meanings in specific situations. Most decisions concern prosaic, everyday conflicts. On Sunday morning, shall I go to church, go fishing, spend the day with my family, or sleep? What shall I do with some windfall money—take a vacation, have the roof of my house repaired, save it, or give it to charity?

Concerning such day-to-day conflicts, Frankl told me: "Take a certain morning. Shall I devote myself to my wife or look up a patient at the hospital? The conflict disappears when I can see that the value of my professional visit for the sake of the sick is of a higher order than just being with my wife. But suppose she needs me because she too is sick. Then the choice seems to be one sick person against another. But there is a difference because in one case I am re-

placeable, and in the other I am not. In the case of my patient at the hospital I can send a member of my staff to look
after him. Such questions as 'Who is replaceable?' and 'Who
is unique in this situation?' carry great weight in deciding
value conflicts.''[4]

Thus the decision again is returned to the individual.
Even though general values help decision making, we still
must decide about the rank of conflicting—or seemingly
conflicting—values; and we also may have to decide when
to take a stand against a widely accepted value. It is important to realize that a value hierarchy, like meaning, cannot
be arbitrarily fabricated. It must be found by personal effort.
It will not do to impose our own order of values on life; we
must find the reality of our lives. Whether reality is placed
there by God or by life is a question we must decide. The
important thing is that a value hierarchy exists and that it is
up to us to find our own.

Even high and universally accepted values must not be
arbitrarily elevated and worshipped out of all proportion.
This is idolatry. Frankl insists that every idolatry carries its
own punishment by leading to despair. And by the same to-
ken every despair is based, in the last analysis, on idolatry
of one value above all others. He quotes his teacher, Rudolf
Allers, as saying that idolatry destroys idol worshippers exactly in that area where they sin against the value hierarchy. In Hitler's Germany the values of "blood and soil"
were raised to the status of an idol and all other values were
subordinated. As a result, Germany lost exactly that—blood
and soil: the blood of her young generation and large parts
of her territory.

5. Our Intuitive Conscience

Conscience is as much a part of man as his leg or arm.

THOMAS JEFFERSON

If no one can "give" us meanings and we cannot fabricate but have to discover them in response to life's demands, how then can we find meanings? The preceding chapter discussed the help we can get from values, but even here we must decide about value priorities. How do we do it? I must admit that Frankl's answers, when I first heard them, were disappointing. But after fifteen years of testing them against my own experiences and those of others in sharing groups, I have concluded his answers are as sound as anything we human beings can come up with.

As far as our knowledge of ultimate meaning is concerned, we have not improved our answers in the five thousand years of written history. Frankl once said that the only answers we have are those of Job (that we do not know) and Socrates (that all we know is that we know nothing). Ultimate meaning remains a basic assumption that can be tested only in daily living: We can live *as if* ultimate meaning exists, then try to live as if everything is chaos and chance, and move in the direction of fulfillment.

To find the meanings of the moments, however, we can have help. We cannot rely on instinct, as primitive people could; and rationality does not help us either. But we have an instrument of meaning discovery buried in our noëtic unconscious. According to Frankl, our conscience alone enables us to find the meaning of a specific situation.

Rediscovery of Conscience

To proclaim conscience as the guide for behavior is not new. It is the oldest answer to one of the oldest questions. It is a *re*discovery that is vital today. Conscience has become a victim of reductionist thinking. Because it cannot be researched in the psychophysical dimension, it has been widely discarded as part of human reality. Conscience is considered the result of a learning process, or it is replaced by the psychodynamic "superego." If we accept these interpretations, we are "ethical" only because we have learned to behave a certain way or because we want to comply with a father image. In this manner a phenomenon existing in the noëtic, that is, in the specifically human dimension, is "explained away" through processes that are part of the lower dimensions of human existence and that disregard the dimension of the spirit. Frankl rejects such interpretations as reductionistic. Conscience as a "specifically human phenomenon" is not the mere consequence of learning processes, father images, or anything else. Although conscience is influenced by training and outside influences, it cannot be reduced to these influences. Frankl defines conscience as an intuitive capacity to find out, to "sniff out" the unique meaning *gestalt* inherent in a situation, "what is meant" in a specific situation.

Frankl illustrates his thesis that conscience is a specifically human phenomenon with the following story: a typical reductionist theory considers the conscience as the outcome of conditioning processes. A dog that has soiled the carpet and slinks under the couch with its tail between its legs acts indeed as a result of conditioning processes. It displays anticipatory anxiety, a fear of getting punished. The human conscience must not be reduced to such a level. As long as human conduct is determined by fear of punishment, hope for rewards, or the wish to comply with the superego, the genuine conscience has not been heard at all *(UC,* pp. 55–56).

He considers it "pseudomorality" when we act moral only because we want to live in peace with our superego. True morality begins only when we make a decision to act for the sake of someone or something, not merely for ourselves—be it to have a clear conscience or to get rid of an irritated superego.

The Rabbi and the Cat

In analyzing human experience Frankl uses the phenomenological method of Husserl and Scheler, which is also the basis of Heidegger's existential philosophy. Frankl defines phenomenology as an approach that describes the actual way we experience the world and ourselves, but without fitting the phenomena of our experiences into preconceived patterns of interpretation—as we do when we do not take human phenomena at their face value but reduce them to a subhuman level. An example of a preconceived pattern of interpretation is the *a priori* assumption that values can be nothing but defense mechanisms and reaction formations, conscience nothing but superego, and love nothing but sex. If we thus exclude in advance the human from the human dimension, we shall never be able to find the human being, only the animal, perhaps only the computer.

Frankl loves the wisdom of Jewish humor and satirizes reductionist behavior with the following story: two men seek a rabbi's judgment. The first claims that the other's cat has eaten his butter. The second denies this. The rabbi asks the first man how much butter the cat has eaten. "Two pounds," answers the man. The rabbi weighs the cat and finds it weighs exactly two pounds. "Now we have found the butter," decides the rabbi, "but where is the cat?" The rabbi argued away the reality of the cat for the sake of a preconceived assumption that if there are two pounds, they must be butter. Similarly, reductionists among behavior therapists assume *a priori* that human behavior can be explained, and explained fully, by our so-called innate releasing mechanisms. "These behaviorists," concludes Frankl, "find the releasing mechanisms—but where is the human being?"[1]

The phenomenological method stresses reality as we experience and observe it—reality as lived, not reduced to satisfy *a priori* assumptions. Conscience, the centerpiece of the noëtic dimension, is as much a part of reality as body and psyche.

To understand the logotherapeutic view we must remember that science first explored our physical dimensions and only later our psychological dimensions. The spirit had no place in a reality so narrowly circumscribed. Science tends to forget that these theoretical concepts are merely ways we can *think* of existence. In *actual* existence we are not *a* body, *a* psyche, *a noös*, but an indivisible unit. Frankl considers this holistic concept of the human being, against the growing pluralism of scientific thought, the most important topic of this age. For this reason he selected this theme in his address to the world elite of scholars at the six-hundredth anniversary of the University of Vienna in 1965. He chose as his title "The Pluralism of Sciences and the Unity of Man."

Conscience is part of human reality. True conscience is not just what parents, religion, or society tell us. These influences are real, but at our core we still have this strange little voice. It plays a central part in our life. How we listen and how we act upon what we hear can make our life meaningful or empty, can cause happiness and fulfillment or tension, conflicts, frustration, and mental disease.

Our Task to Listen

The rediscovery of an authentic human conscience has practical consequences. First, we must listen. It may well be that the most important task that will bring meaning is to listen to our conscience. We act as humans only if we act because we have decided to and not because we are driven to it or because we are afraid of punishment. It is true that commandments and laws threaten punishment; but as long as we live according to them automatically, we have ruled ourselves out as persons, as selves. The Ten Commandments are among the best guidelines we have, but routine obedience is not enough. As Frankl states, "In an age when the Ten Commandments seem to lose their unconditional validity, we have to learn more than ever to listen to the ten thousand commandments arising from the ten thousand unique situations of which life consists" *(WM,* pp. 64-65), in order to understand the tens of thousands of unique meanings offered by the tens of thousands of moments that make up our life.

Occasionally, and increasingly, the advice of our conscience contradicts an accepted value, even one of the Ten Commandments (as in the example of Frankl's saying good-bye to his wife in Auschwitz). Without a conscience, rules and regulations would be our only guidelines. But rules by their very nature are too rigid and general to fit unique situations. They work under normal circumstances, but in fast-changing times they become outdated. They tend to suffocate us unless we accept them by our own free will, responsibly, not arbitrarily. We must listen to our inner ear, which picks up whispers of ultimate meanings and a hierarchy of values otherwise inaccessible. The imagery has changed significantly: in biblical times our ancestors behaved morally for fear of an eye in the sky; today we behave morally because we listen to an ear within. The eye in the sky was an inescapable outside threat, but it is now our decision to pay attention to our inner ear. We can turn it off when we wish. We are free to move with or against our spiritual voice. We can be browbeaten, persuaded, hypnotized, brainwashed, or shamed into honoring our father and mother; but the human way is free choice.

We do take a risk by following our conscience. Frankl is careful to point out that our conscience, being genuinely human, also has that typically human ability to err: It cannot only guide us, it may mislead us. Even more, we never know, not even on our deathbed, whether it has been the true meaning to which we committed ourselves. But although our conscience may err, we have to obey it. The possibility of error does not release us from the necessity of trying (*WM*, p. 65). The thought that we have to risk error was also forcefully expressed by Gordon W. Allport, professor of psychology at Harvard University: "We can be at one and the same time half-sure and whole-hearted."[2]

Conscience in Hitler's Germany

Greater than the risk of an erring conscience is the risk of a suppressed conscience. Under drastic circumstances it may make someone an Eichmann or a Hitler. Frankl is often asked about the conscience of the Germans under national socialism: did it tell them to betray their fathers and mothers for the sake of the state, to plunder Jewish stores, and to commit mass murder? Frankl's answer is that he does not believe Hitler ever obeyed his conscience. Never can one's true conscience, he says, command one to do what Hitler did. "I am convinced that Hitler would never have become what he did unless he had supressed within himself the voice of conscience" (*WM*, p. 66).

Hitler's Germany also illustrates what can happen if conscience becomes the result of indoctrination by a dictator. The German tragedy lay in the fact that the German people confused the state ideology with their personal conscience. If they had listened to their conscience, they could have decided in every case whether to follow the voice of their conscience or that of the propaganda machinery. Some did follow the voice of their conscience, dangerous as it was in the times of the Third Reich. Rabbi Harold Schulweis of Los Angeles several years ago founded the Institute for the Righteous Acts, devoted to finding Germans who risked their lives to help and hide Jews and other victims of the Nazi regime. The institute found a number of such "righteous" men and women, some martyred by the Nazis, some still alive. Frankl knows of some who, following the dictates of their conscience, joined the resistance movement, were imprisoned in concentration camps, and died there. On his U.S. lecture tours he is sometimes asked why he returned to Vienna after his concentration camp experiences. He then tells of the Catholic baroness who at great peril hid one of Frankl's cousins during the war years or of the socialist attorney he had known only slightly who supplied him with potatoes and tomatoes in 1942 when food was severely rationed and any contact with Jews was dangerous. These were exceptions, but so were the murderers and robbers. Frankl rejects the concept of collective guilt. If there was "guilt," it was about the "crime" of remaining passive, of having heard but not acted upon the voice of their conscience. He mentions a well-known Viennese actress who had been forced by Hitler's minister, Josef Goebbels, to accept the lead in a Nazi propaganda movie. Many people later expressed the view that she should have refused, even at the risk of being sent to a concentration camp, rather than lend prestige and popularity to the Hitler cause. In principle Frankl agrees but feels such extreme heroism can be demanded only by those who proved by their own actions that they chose the concentration camp rather than collaboration. And he observes that actual survivors of the camps tend to be more tolerant than others because they know the full import of such a decision.

Frankl concludes that he prefers living in a world in

which we are challenged to choose our own existence, a world, that is, in which such phenomena as Hitler and a saint can coexist. He prefers such a world to one in which there is nothing but complete conformism and collectivism, where everyone is forced by either a state or a party, to act in a certain way.

The Risk of Uncertainty

The voice of conscience speaks to us, but we are free to say no. This is our choice: to listen and follow as best we can or to surrender our freedom and consider ourselves driven by forces beyond our control. Thus we are not determined by conscience but led, and sometimes misled, by it. This is another consequence of the rediscovery of a highly personal conscience: the awareness that we must make our choices in the face of ultimate uncertainty. We must accept the fact that we do not have the capacity to grasp universal order and meaning with our rational mind and that the only way to glimpse them is through our intuitive and possibly erring conscience. We have to face the fact that we must constantly make decisions on the basis of incomplete evidence. Columbus never would have discovered America had he waited for all the information on which to base his decision to start out on his journey. Few people would decide on a career, marriage, or parenthood if they waited until all the information was in.

There are positive aspects about this uncertainty. Because we cannot be certain our conscience in a specific situation has led us in the right direction, we cannot be certain that someone else's conscience in the same situation has not led its owner somewhere else. Others may understand the meaning of a situation more clearly than we do. Such an attitude, warns Frankl, must not lead to indifference but to tolerance. Indifference would mean that everyone is right.

That is nonsense. "There is only one meaning in a situation but no one can know if you have found it, and not someone else." This leads to tolerance. "Being tolerant does not mean that I share another one's belief. But it does mean that I acknowledge another one's right to believe, and obey, his own conscience" (*WM*, p. 66).

Nevertheless, the question keeps coming up whether there are no general guidelines to indicate whether conscience is leading us in the right direction. In many of my group discussions there has been a consensus that under normal circumstances we are justified in being suspicious of a conscience that steers its owner away from cooperation and toward hostile competition, away from wholeness and belonging toward separation and alienation, or away from life toward death.

The Presence of Conflicts

If we see our conscience as a guiding voice that can say no to government, society, inner drives, parents, spouses, our upbringing, and our past, then conflicts are unavoidable. Every moment brings choice; every choice brings conflicts; every conflict brings tension. To Frankl tensions are inherent in the human condition: tensions between what we are and what our conscience tells us to be, between our reality and our ideals. To reduce this kind of tension would rob us of our humanness. Tension can sharpen our conscience. A guilty conscience can be a gift if it leads to higher self-criticism, better self-understanding, and self-improvement.

One does not need to be around Frankl long before becoming aware that he is listening to his conscience, sometimes with surprising results. After a lecture in Palo Alto, California, he was told that a prisoner in San Quentin had read *Man's Search for Meaning* and that it had changed his entire outlook on life. The director of San Quentin had heard Frankl was in the area and asked if it would be possible for him to see the prisoner. To the consternation of all who had arranged his California trip, Frankl reshuffled his schedule to allow for the visit to San Quentin. Another time a film company in Hollywood offered him cash for a movie option on a book. He insisted on seeing some of the company's productions (which were full of violence and sensationalism) and refused the offer. Sometimes he can be rude in compliance with his conscience. On his American lecture tours he almost always refuses dinner invitations or even short chats over cups of coffee because he feels that working on or simply resting in preparation for a lecture is more important to his life task than social obligations. (The European style of social life allows for more privacy.) But then again he can be extremely tolerant of someone else's conscience. When I was in Vienna after a twenty-seven-year absence, he set aside an evening to give me an added opportunity to discuss some questions. The date conflicted with a *Burgtheater* performance of a play I had wanted to see (and he knew how I missed the Vienna theater in the United States). I felt embarrassed to cancel our interview in favor of a play, but he immediately agreed, facetiously using his own terminology: "This is the only time this play is being shown during your stay here. This is a unique opportunity; for you this is the meaning of the situation. We can have the talk tomorrow."

Logotherapeutic Dream Interpretation

Conflicts of conscience may have serious consequences and in some instances lead to noögenic neuroses. Just as the psychoanalyst attempts to make patients conscious of repressed drives, so the logotherapist will help make patients conscious of their repressed spiritual conflicts, such as conflicts of conscience.

Like repressed drives, the repressed voice of conscience

will sometimes reveal itself in dreams. The psychoanalyst looks to dreams for manifestations of the instinctual unconscious; the logotherapist looks for telltale signs from the spiritual unconscious. Logotherapy, too, uses free associations for dream interpretation. Frankl sees this relationship between the two schools of therapy in these terms: "We march together, but we fight different battles."

The conscience may speak through dreams to warn us of dangers we do not see in our wakeful state or confront us with self-criticism we do not face consciously. Frankl provides an example of each in *The Unconscious God:*

A woman dreamed that, along with her dirty wash, she took a dirty cat to the laundry. When she came to pick up the laundry she found the cat dead. She came up with the following free associations: As to "cat," she said that she loved cats above all; but equally she loved her daughter—her only child—"above all." From this we may infer that "cat" stands for "child." But why is the cat "dirty"? That became clear when we learned from the patient that recently she had been worrying about the gossip surrounding her daughter's love life—her "dirty linen," too, was being washed in public. That was the reason why the patient, as she admitted, was constantly watching and hounding her daughter. The dream expressed a warning to the patient not to torment her daughter with exaggerated demands for moral "cleanliness" or she might lose her child [*UG,* p. 41].

To this interpretation Frankl comments, "We cannot see any reason why we should give up such straightforward interpretation, open to whatever presents itself in the dream, in deference to the preconceived idea that behind it infantile-sexual contents *must* be hidden."

Another example in *The Unconscious God* is a dream of repressed self-criticism.

The patient reports a dream that kept recurring, even within one night. He would dream that he was in another city and wanted to phone a certain lady. But the dial was so gigantic—it contained some hundred numbers—that he never succeeded in placing the call. After waking, the patient realized that the number he meant to dial was not the lady's but that of a record company for which he was then working with great financial success as a composer of popular music. In the discussion of the dream it turned out that he had actually spent a very satisfying time in the city he dreamed of, composing religious music, whereas his present work, although outwardly successful, did not give him inner fulfillment. Except for his composing, he cherished no pleasant memories connected with that city. In particular, he had no longing for the lady, with whom he never had an erotic relationship. On the other hand, he spontaneously declared that the gigantic dial signified the trouble he had when choosing. (To understand the symbolism of the dream we have to realize that in German the same word, *wählen*, is used for "choosing" and "dialing.") What, then, was the patient's choice? It did not refer to a number to dial but rather the vocation to choose—specifically, to the choice between keeping a well-paying, unsatisfying job as a composer of hits or writing religious music. Suddenly the essential meaning of the dream became clear. Although in vain, the patient had been struggling to be "connected" again, to be "reconnected." Now we just have to replace *reconnexio* by *religio*, which in Latin means the same, and it is obvious that the dream expressed the patient's desire to find his way back to his true religious and artistic vocation [*UG*, pp. 41–42].

Frankl comments, "This dream, unlike the previous one, does not present a warning to the dreamer but rather expresses a self-reproach. In both cases, however, the dream is an utterance of conscience—in the second case, not only of ethical conscience but also of the artistic conscience; but both dreams are expressions of the spiritual conscience."

A Voice from the Unconscious

As mentioned, our intuitive conscience can make accessible meanings that are closed to the rational approach. An illustration of the way Frankl sees the conscience work is found in *Psychotherapy and Existentialism:*

Shortly before the United States entered World War II, I was called to the American Consulate in Vienna to receive my immigration visa. My old parents expected me to leave Austria as soon as the visa was given. However, at the last moment I hesitated: the question of whether I should leave my parents beset me. I knew that any day they could be taken to a concentration camp. Shouldn't I stay with them? While pondering this question I found that this was the type of dilemma which made one wish for a hint from Heaven. It was then that I noticed a piece of marble lying on a table at home. When I asked my father about it, he explained that he had found it on the site where the National Socialists had burned down the largest Viennese synagogue. My father had taken this marble piece home because it was a part of the tablets which contained the Ten Commandments. The piece showed one engraved and gilded Hebrew letter. My father explained that this letter was the abbreviation for only one of the Commandments. Eagerly I asked, "Which one is it?" The answer was: "Honor thy father and thy mother: that thy days may be long upon the land." So I stayed with my father and my mother upon the land and decided to let the American visa lapse.

Acknowledging this piece of marble as a hint from Heaven might well be the expression of the fact that already long before, in the depth of my heart, I had decided to stay. I only projected this decision into the appearance of the marble piece. Much the same way would it be self-expression if one saw nothing but $CaCO_3$ in it—although I would call this rather a projection of an existential vacuum [*PE*, pp. 34–35].

Frankl will never know whether his decision was right. One may argue that it was a futile gesture or that it helped him become the human being he is now. The intuitive quality of conscience always points beyond reason into a dimension where reality not merely "is" but changes by the very fact of our decision.

In one respect Frankl compares conscience with love: Love sees the potentialities of the beloved that have not yet been actualized. These potentialities are unique and so elude the grasp of pure reason—we can only seize them by intuition. Similarly, conscience makes us aware of the meaning potentials of a situation not yet actualized, thus making reality out of what might otherwise have remained an unfulfilled possibility.

An Instrument of Human Progress

This interpretation of conscience as a personal, intuitive outreach into the world of unique meaning potentialities makes it ultimately the instrument of human progress. Conscience stands up to authority, law, society, and all outside influences and sees something fresh behind old truths. It is a long way from a society that accepted cannibalism as moral (and probably of religious significance) to one in which young people risk social ostracism for refusing to kill even enemies in war. One can imagine a father in a primitive tribe telling his son who refused to eat the flesh of other human beings: "Don't sin against God. He wouldn't have made people out of flesh if he had not wanted us to eat them." Yet the son would refuse. In discussing such a hypothetical incident, Frankl declared,

> In a society that universally accepted cannibalism, only a person with an exceedingly refined conscience would have been able to contradict the environment in which he was brought up. When that person's conscience contradicted cannibalism, he became a revolutionary. He may have been killed, but he was able to awaken the conscience of others. This is the way human progress takes place. And in particular, this is the way revolutions are started—and religions founded.[3]

Admittedly, progress is desperately slow as measured in one person's life. People take a long time to act according to what they know is right. Most signers of the Declaration of Independence, which named liberty among our inalienable rights, owned slaves. The mills of conscience, one might say, grind exceedingly slowly; and it is often impossible to decide for a long time whether they produce wheat or chaff. We live in times of "conscientious objections"—against war, too much government power, taxes, and race, sex, and age discrimination. Whether these are spurred on by true or deceived consciences only time will tell. At present, objectors cannot know for certain whether they are sound revolutionaries or nonconformists defying society. Yet they have to follow their consciences as best they can, sharpening their ears to hear its voices and to be tolerant toward the actions of others who, after all, are also following their consciences. This is not easily done in our age of science, when human progress is measured in data that can be counted, calculated, fed into computers, and analyzed. But computers can only tell us how people behave on the average and in sample groups, never how an individual ought to behave in specific situations. Our life is not regulated at every crossing by a red light that tells us to stop or a green light that tells us to go ahead. We live in an era of flashing yellow lights that leave the decision to the individual.

6. *The Essence of Humanness*

In logotherapy the pursuit of meaning is more than an inalienable right—it is the essence of humanness. If we repress it, we open up in ourselves the infernal pit of the existential vacuum. If we devote ourselves to this pursuit, our
lives are filled with meaning and the by-products of a
meaningful existence: happiness, security, peace of mind,
mental stability, and such currently fashionable life goals as
self-actualization and peak experiences. All these, logotherapy claims, will elude us if we consciously set out to gain
them; but they will fall into our lap as unintended results of
our search for meaning.

Pursuit of Happiness: A Self-Contradiction

These happy consequences of our pursuit of meaning become clear when we see human beings, as Frankl does, not
as closed systems but as reaching out, beyond themselves, to
a world of fellow beings and meanings, who provide us
with a reason to be happy. Happiness *en*sues if we have a
reason to be happy (*PE*, p. 41). If, on the other hand, we *pur*-
sue happiness, it becomes the objective of our motivation
and, worse, the object of our attention. To the degree to
which this takes place we can no longer be happy. It is the

pursuit of *meaning* that counts. The pursuit of happiness amounts to a self-contradiction: the more it is pursued, the less it is attained (*UG*, p. 85).

In "Beyond Self-Expression and Self-Actualization," Frankl explains his thesis in terms of other phenomena that escape when intentionally pursued. A direct effort to fall asleep makes us tense and sleepless. If we are overly concerned with our health, we are already sick with hypochondria. If we are preoccupied with prestige, we will meet contempt as a status seeker. If we act "good" only to have a good conscience, we are a hypocrite; good conscience is a by-product of *being* good.

In sexual neuroses, for example, Frankl proves that happiness escapes the seeker who directly pursues it. If a man is intent on demonstrating potency and a woman on demonstrating her ability to experience orgasm, they may fail. It is precisely the pursuit of sexual happiness, he says, the direct attempt to experience pleasure, that dooms it to failure. The same is true for happiness in general. What people really want, Frankl says, is not happiness but a reason to be happy. In neuroses, the search for a reason is deflected into a direct pursuit of happiness, a will to pleasure. Pleasure becomes the direct aim of a forced intention, the sole content of attention. The more pleasure is the center of our attention, the less attention we pay to the reasons that may cause us pleasure. In chasing after happiness, we chase it away (*WM*, p. 33 ff.).

I experienced this self-defeating nature of happiness intentionally pursued when, on my first visit to the Alps in twenty-seven years, I tried to recapture the happiness I had felt in my youth, hiking in the mountains filled with wild flowers and bird songs. I joined a hiking group led by a naturalist going to my favorite mountain area. We were walking single file, constantly looking out for rare specimens. Every few moments the naturalist would stop at a flower, gather the entire group around him, and lecture. Or he would tiptoe to a tree, forefinger on lips, pointing to a bird on a branch. I learned much about birds and flowers but could not recapture the joy that filled me on the hikes I had taken merely for the sake of experiencing the beauty of nature. It was a case of one bird in the hand being worth less than two left singing in the bushes.

From Aristotle to Jefferson, happiness has been regarded as the principal goal of life and its pursuit central to human existence. Freud made the pleasure principle a central force of human motivation; but Frankl sides with Immanuel Kant and Max Scheler, who warned that pleasure is not an aim but a side effect. Happiness, pleasure, and peak experiences are always the same, even though the reasons for them may differ widely. But as Frankl points out, no one can isolate happiness from its reasons. He quotes Abraham Maslow: "In the real world there is no such thing as blushing without something to blush about."[1] Only in context, Maslow says, is blushing possible. Similarly, Frankl adds, only in context is happiness possible—the context of a reason to be happy. We cannot find a relationship with happiness itself, only with actions and people giving us happiness in devotion to a person or a task.

Casual students of logotherapy sometimes object to the idea that happiness comes only in response to a task. Happiness, they say, comes and goes as it pleases and often at the most unexpected moments—while walking alone in a thunderstorm or watching the waves break against rocks or lying in a meadow with a beloved person. These critics overlook the fact that meaning and happiness come not only as the result of activity, or "tasks" in a narrow sense, but also as the result of an experience, be it aesthetic, intellectual, or emotional. One of the three categories of values Frankl distinguishes is "experiential values," realized whenever we enjoy nature or culture or experience beauty, truth, or love.

Reasons and Causes for Happiness

In Berkeley, where interest in the pursuit of happiness via drugs is high, Frankl was asked what he thought about inducing pleasure and peak experiences by artificial means such as drugs, "happiness pills," and alcohol. His answer is that they can never be a "reason" for our happiness, but they may be a cause. Reason implies a psychological relationship, but cause is strictly physiological-biochemical. When someone is weeping because she lost a friend, she has a reason; but when someone is weeping while cutting an onion, the onion is not a reason for his tears—it is a cause. Happiness, too, can be induced by a cause—by pills and even an electric current. Frankl tells of an experiment where electrodes were implanted in a certain spot in the brains of rats, and every time a rat pushed a lever, the animal experienced sexual pleasure or the pleasure resulting from food intake. The rats eventually pressed the lever thousands of times a day and neglected the real food and their real sex partner. That is the way people behave who use causes rather than reasons to experience pleasure. The causes may well be chemical but the reasons must be human.[2]

Alcohol, Frankl suspects, may be popular today because people, unable to find reasons for happiness in their objective world, are looking for causes they can fabricate. He illustrated that point with a joke. A deaf patient is told by his doctor to stop drinking whiskey. Two months later he is cured of deafness, but at the next visit the patient is as deaf as before. He is drinking again. "Listen," he explains to his doctor, "first I was drinking and my hearing became worse. Then I stopped drinking and heard better. But what I heard was not as good as whiskey." Frankl commented, "Lacking a meaning that would have been a reason for happiness, he tried to find happiness directly, with the help of chemistry, by-passing meaning (*WM*, pp. 36–37).

Self-Actualization

Self-actualization—another concept that, with peak experiences, has become popular through modern psychological literature—is desirable but can be achieved only to the extent to which we fulfill the concrete meaning of a specific situation. If we seek self-actualization for its own sake, we will not attain it. To support this point, Frankl quotes two men who lived twenty-five hundred years apart. The ancient Greek poet Pindar admonished us in one of the earliest samples of existential advice to "become what you are." The contemporary existentialist Karl Jaspers supplements Pindar by stating, "What man is he has become through that cause which he has made his own."[3]

Frankl goes a step further and asks when we are most concerned with self-actualization. His answer is when our pursuit of meaning is frustrated. A boomerang presented to him in Australia seemed to him a symbol for human existence and its transcending quality. It is not the boomerang's job to return to the hunter, but to kill the prey. The boomerang returns only if it missed the target. Similarly, we also only return to ourselves, are concerned with ourselves, after we missed our mission and failed to find a meaning in life (*PE*, p. 9).

Charlotte Bühler has said that people who speak of self-actualization really mean the fulfillment of their potentials.[4] Seen in this manner, our life task would be to actualize as many of our potentials as possible. But if we would blindly actualize our potentials, we would feel neither self-actualized nor happy. We must evaluate our potentials and select among them with a direction in mind. The "pursuit" of meaning implies choice of direction. Frankl quotes Socrates as having said that he had many potentials, including the potential to be a criminal. By actualizing this potential, the great defender of law and justice would have become a common criminal. Frankl's point is supported by everyday experience. There are many ways to be happy (to love someone or to dominate), many ways to actualize creativity (to create symphonies or atom bombs), and many ways of self-realization (to realize our artistic or our practical self, our cruel streak or our compassion). Thus to "What am I able to do?" must be added the second question, "What am I called to do?" Here our freedom of choice must be tempered by responsibleness, and this is made more difficult by the fact that we rarely get a second chance. Frankl, in *Psychotherapy and Existentialism*, stresses that at every moment several potentials present themselves to us. It is not enough to actualize them; we must choose and thus make one of them part of reality or condemn all the others to nonbeing. Decisions are final. Once actualized, what once was a potential can no longer be withdrawn. The consequences cannot be foreseen. Each life situation provides the burdensome challenge of selecting the potentials we decide to make real. Here, too, we have only our conscience to guide us, human and prone to error as it may be.

Healthy Tensions

The necessity to make choices of meaning, values, and priority leads to tensions; but these are healthy tensions. We are well advised to avoid physical and psychological tensions, but logotherapy regards the tensions of the spirit as healthy. They result from stretching from what we are to what we have the vision of becoming. In Frankl's view, to be human means to be caught in the tension between what we are and what we are meant to be, to be aware that we do not need to remain the way we are but can always change (*PE*, p. 37ff.).

He opposed current motivational theories that hold we are primarily concerned with maintaining or regaining inner equilibrium and, to this end, with reducing tensions. He quotes Charlotte Bühler, who points out that from Freud's early formulation of the pleasure principle to the current version of the homeostasis principle the goal of all human activities has been the restoration of equilibrium (*PE*, p. 37). She doubts Freud's assumption (based on the physical knowledge of his time) that the release of tension is the sole primary tendency of life. Frankl maintains that reality is then reduced to a mere means to an end, namely to satisfy our drives and all things and all people have then only the purpose to serve as means to an end, namely to meet a need and to achieve a state of equilibrium (*WM*, p. 31 ff.).

Given such a view, parents raise children to spare them conflicts; teachers do not challenge their students but help them adjust; people go to church (or to the analyst) to find peace of mind; they form friendships to satisfy a need; or they do good deeds to get rid of a bad conscience. Everything is done for the sake of inner equilibrium. Everything is devaluated to the level of mere means to achieve a tensionless state. This striving for equilibrium, according to Frankl, is expressed by patients suffering from sexual neuroses. They speak of "masturbating on a woman." Such men use their partner simply for the purpose of reducing sexual tension. A healthy person will not see others in what Martin Buber called an "I-it relationship," where people are not seen as persons to be encountered but as things to be used.

That meaning and values are within us and all we need to do is "realize our inner self" is a popular but dangerous view. It is popular because it absolves us of the effort to reach out for values—they are already in us. It is dangerous for the same reason: If we do not reach out and are content with attaining such inner conditions as Maslow's "self-actualization" and "peak experiences," we end in Frankl's "abyss experience" of meaninglessness. To raise us from the abyss, logotherapy prescribes a certain healthy dose of tension, for instance the tension between the demand of a meaning and the efforts to respond to it. In a deeper sense Frankl sees the tension between being and meaning as fundamental: "Meaning always must be one step ahead of Being—only then can meaning fulfill its own meaning, namely to be the pacemaker of Being" (PE, p. 12).

The Pacemakers and the Peacemakers

Frankl illustrates the concept of pacemaker in *Psychotherapy and Existentialism* with a logotherapeutic interpretation of the Exodus story, when God led the tribe of Israel through the wilderness into the promised land. God, the Bible says, floated ahead of the Israelites in the form of a cloud. God led them, was their pacemaker. The wanderers in the wilderness would never have been able to find their way into the promised land if the cloud had not stayed ahead of them but had settled among them. The cloud would have ceased to be a leader and become a fog.

One could go a step further and speculate that human progress is based on the vision of godhead as pacemaker. An anthropology student at the University of California developed the theory that our primitive ancestors never would have found the courage to domesticate and ride a horse without the vision of swiftness they attributed to their gods of the hunt. Because the fastest animal they knew was the wild horse, they imagined the gods on the back of the fastest, wildest horses. Only after they had become accustomed to the idea of such an image could they conceive the thought of seeing themselves on horseback. Once human beings conceive a goal, they find the courage to reach for it. The gods have always been the example, the ultimate force that coaxes us along to do what first were impossible dreams. People have always endowed their gods with qualities they long for: to fly through the air, destroy their enemies, or conquer disease and death. Thus they pictured their gods as winged, powerful, and eternal. And, following the eternal pacemaker, they have managed to make many of their dreams come true. We now fly faster than Mercury and are approaching the destructive power of Jahweh; we have conquered many diseases and talk of old age as if one day it, too, will be conquered. Yet some qualities of the pacemaker remain unreached, perhaps unreachable: to know truth, to be just and wise, to know good from evil, to know life's ultimate meaning.

God's quality as pacemaker has itself become a human goal. Religious leaders, poets, explorers, philosophers, teachers, and parents have all wanted to be, and often were, pacemakers. Recently, however, a generation has grown up that is pursuing a different goal: not that of pacemakers, but "peacemakers," although not in the sense the Bible uses the word when speaking of the "blessed peacemakers" who shall be called "the children of God." Frankl sees pacemakers as confronting us with challenges and peacemakers as stressing peace of mind at any price, trying to spare us confrontations. Moses was a pacemaker. He never attempted to make it easy for his people; he brought the Ten Commandments to the Israelites and not only confronted them with high ideals but pointed out to them how far short they fell.

Peacemakers, as Frankl portrays them, take the opposite approach. Concerned with inner equilibrium, they do not confront us with uncomfortable ideals, but with facts. They do not make us stretch our vistas, but assure us that everything is fine the way it is. They try to persuade us that meanings are within, that we need not bother reaching out, that adjustment, not reaching, is the goal in life. Today's peacemakers think not in terms of ideals but of normalcy; they trust not in hopes and dreams but in statistics and opinion polls. They talk about the "average" person instead of the unique individual, but the average person can find no meaning because there is no average meaning. The peacemakers supply facts that comfort the majority: "Why bother with ideals? Why differ from the average? If most husbands cheat on their wives, why be faithful? If most people lie, why be truthful?" The goal of the peacemakers is to make people not good, wise, or just but "normal." It is an ironic twist of language that from this point of view most present-day warmakers must be classified as "peacemakers." They do not think of war's effect on human beings and values; they think in terms of logistics, efficiency of destruction, and cost per enemy killed. In an effort to "adjust to the facts of life" they accept the standards of the enemy they are fighting.

The United States at its founding was a pacemaker for the entire Western world. The new country was an example in democracy, individualism, freedom, and personal responsibility. The resulting upsurge of optimism and purposefulness lasted more than a century. Now, however, the United States has become a peacemaker, concerned with equilibrium. The ideals of democracy have been frozen into a worship of the *status quo*. The Declaration of Independence is a revered document, no longer a living example. Individual freedom has become entangled in bureaucracy. The responsibility of decision making has been transferred from the individual to the anonymity of committees, organizations, and government agencies. The country's shift from pacemaker (concerned with values) to peacemaker (concerned with facts) may well account for the widespread feeling of apathy and meaninglessness. Americans sense the loss of values and ideals of their country's founders, pacemakers of liberation and revolution. In those days the United States was a revolutionary country in a conservative world. Today the United States is a conservative country in a revolutionary world. But a *status quo* society has no challenge, only equilibrium. Its goals are pleasure and power, not ideals and meanings. Mere lip service is given to independence, individual responsibleness, inventiveness, ambition, and honesty. A new set of goals has emerged, among which are bigness, material well-being, *status quo*, social security, a well-balanced personality, and a good image.

There is evidence, however, that American youth long for their country to become a pacemaker again. This found expression during the Kennedy administration, which challenged the American people to respond to individual tasks. "Ask not what your country can do for you; ask what you can do for your country," he demanded. It is unlikely that President Kennedy ever came across Frankl's first American book, *The Doctor and the Soul;* but there the thought is: "Man should not ask what he may expect from life, but should rather understand that life expects something from him" *(DS, p. xi).* That Kennedy's appeal fell on fertile ground was obvious by the response of America's youth to the Peace Corps. For the United States to become a pacemaker again, however, will require the application of the "power of the human spirit" by thousands of individuals to overcome the *status quo* mindedness that has frozen the old values in all three branches of government.

Meaning in the Affluent Society

Trying to answer the puzzle of why our affluent society is beset by a vague feeling of meaninglessness, one is tempted to doubt another one of our most persistent "pursuits"—utopia, the ultimate in affluence and tensionlessness. History supports Frankl's view that complete satisfaction of human needs leads to frustration and an inner void. The Pilgrims, facing a strange and hostile continent, did not feel an existential vacuum; they had a task to fulfill. Societies under stress produce people who find meaning in overcoming their difficulties—from the Israelites wandering in the wilderness to the French under German occupation in World War II. Boredom and emptiness are prevalent in times of plenty and material security—among the freemen of the Roman Empire at the peak of its power, among the aristocrats at the court of Louis XVI, and now among the prosperous in affluent America. The social critic Lewis Mumford put it in resounding words: "The expanding American economy for all its suffocating abundance of machine-made goods and gadgets has resulted in a dismally contracted life, lived for the most part confined to a car or a television set; a life so empty of vivid firsthand experiences that it might as well be lived in a space capsule, traveling from nowhere to nowhere at supersonic speeds."[5] Thirty years ago the Viennese logotherapist Paul Polak warned against the belief that neuroses would disappear when we had solved our economic problems. Polak predicted that only then would the existential questions rise to the top of our consciousness.

This is apparently happening in the affluent societies of the West. Some of the oldest tensions, those caused by the struggle to find food, shelter, and protection against a hostile nature, have been drastically reduced; others, under the influence of the peacemakers, are adjusted, pampered, and tranquilized away. Yet people do not become happier. The strange thing is, observes Frankl, that if they are spared tensions, they create them, either in a healthy or an unhealthy way. The most popular way to create healthy tensions, he thinks, is sports: no other animal puts up hurdles in order to jump over them or climbs rocks simply to overcome the difficulty. But tensions may be built up in many unhealthy ways, too. Young people, particularly if they are not confronted sufficiently with tasks, invent dangerous "sports."

They defy authority, provoke the police, play hooky from school, commit senseless crimes, become vandals, and risk their lives without good reason by "playing chicken." The existential vacuum of youth need not be filled with destructive contents, as was demonstrated in Oslo, Norway, where youthful hooligans who had satisfied their desire for tension by slashing tires and streetcar seats formed a patrol to prevent such activities of competing gangs. To their own surprise, they found it just as "exciting" to be on the side of the law as to fight it.

A Return to Ideals

On visits to the United States Frankl is understandably hesitant to criticize the host country, but he has on occasion commented on the American hankering for a tensionless society. He is aware how much Freud's misunderstood and often uncritically accepted theories have contributed to this utopian dream. In the *Journal of Humanistic Psychology* Frankl points out that Freud's era was one of tension, especially tension aroused by the widespread repression of sex. This, thanks to Freud, has been released, to the great relief of the Anglo-Saxon countries long suffering from the restrictions of a Puritan heritage. In a mass reaction against the unrealistic overdemand of Puritan "virtues" Americans went on a rampage of "underdemand." They became afraid of demanding too much of their young and developed a system of education that carefully refrained from challenging students with "Puritan" concepts such as ideals and values. Frankl calls this "a case of dumping the baby with the bath water." Not only Puritan ideals but *all* ideals were dismissed as outdated. It is considered "twentieth century" to be factual and materialistic. But Frankl sees a return to the challenge of ideals.

In post-Watergate America the widespread demand for

morality in government is making inroads into the comfortable stand of "everybody-is-cheating-why-not-I." President Carter was elected on the strength of an idealism the voters perceived. His fight for universal human rights, considered quixotic by many people abroad, is supported at home. Traditional depth psychology, concerned with needs, is supplemented by an ideal-centered "height psychology," a term Frankl used for logotherapy as far back as 1938. He quotes a "height psychologist" as saying, "Ideals are the very stuff of life" *(WM, p. 47)*. The man who said this is a true "height" psychologist—John H. Glenn, the first American astronaut, a scientist, and now a senator. Ideals are becoming respectable again.

Reducing meanings and values to psychologically and sociologically determined projections of one's inner makeup could not erode the natural idealism of young America. American youth is committed to many causes, from a war on poverty to a fight against nuclear reactors and ecological pollution. Is it unhealthy for students to march and ministers to demonstrate? Yes, if it is done to run away from their existential vacuum, no, if it is done to give life a worthy content. The chief of the psychiatric clinic of the student hospital at the University of California, Berkeley, disclosed that admission to the clinic dropped to almost zero at the time of the student free-speech demonstrations but increased again as soon as the demonstrations were over. Here is support for the thesis that mental health depends on having a meaning to fulfill, an ideal to strive for.

The times are full of challenges. Even in an affluent society we need not look far for tasks to fulfill. Addressing students at the University of Oslo, Frankl concluded, "No one needs to complain about a lack of meanings; you only have to widen your horizon to see that we live in affluence, but others suffer want. We enjoy freedom, but where is our responsibility toward others? Thousands of years ago we developed a belief in One God, a belief in monotheism—but where is our awareness of One Humankind, an awareness of what I might call Monanthropism? An awareness that we are all members of one humanity regardless of color, religion, and political beliefs."[6]

7. Our Crumbling Traditions

Things most taken for granted need most to be doubted.... Don't
let yourself be hypnotized by traditional solutions.

PIET HEIN

Logotherapy maintains that today's widespread feeling of
emptiness is the result of a double loss: the loss of our instincts and our traditions. Animals get direction for their
behavior through instincts. Our ancestors were deprived of
their basic animal instincts long before the beginning of
history. Instinctual security is closed to us forever. We do
not have the salmon's drive to the mountain spring of its
origins nor the bear's impulse toward the warm cave when
winter is threatening. We must find the direction of our
lives by trying to find, from moment to moment, the meaning of our existence. To do this we must rely on values
handed down from generation to generation, by tradition,
through such human institutions as family, church, school,
and state.

Periods of Rapid Change

In times of little change tradition is a reliable guide.
However, in some periods our trust in traditions and institutions breaks down and anxiety results. Paul Tillich, in *The
Courage to Be*, lists three sources of anxiety: death (the fear of
nothingness), guilt (the awareness of having violated a moral law), and meaninglessness (the raising of questions for

which no answer can be be found). Tillich points out that at the end of antiquity people were concerned with the fear of death, and Christianity emerged, offering comfort through immortality and resurrection. At the end of the Middle Ages people were concerned with guilt, and the Reformation offered a way to forgiveness and atonement. Now, at the end of our times, as we enter the nuclear/space age, we suffer from anxiety caused by a feeling of meaninglessness. Conceivably, our concern with meaning could give birth to a new movement, possibly based on existentialism—theological, atheistic, psychological, or some other form.

At the end of each of the three periods—antiquity, the Middle Ages, and modern times—long-accepted values were questioned; established institutions lost their power; and traditions were mistrusted. Possibly this breakdown is more virulent today than in previous transition periods. For the first time the differences between the old and the new are so enormous that mere changes in quantity amount to changes in quality. For instance, we have developed a long string of weapons, each one deadlier than the last. But the H-bomb is more than a new weapon; it is a new way of life and death, forcing us to take a new look at such ancient concepts as war and peace, courage, honor, loyalty, and patriotism. Space travel is not merely another means of transportation but literally opens up the universe, expanding our views of ourselves, of life, and of divinity. We have always assumed responsibility for those close to us; but the atomic age, with its radioactive wastes and an industrialization that pollutes our natural resources, forces us to assume responsibility for generations we shall never know. This is a challenge religion and philosophy never faced. We are now required to love our neighbor ten generations hence. Kant's categorical imperative would challenge us to act on maxims we would accept as universal laws five thousand years from now; and Buber's I-Thou relationships would extend far beyond their present concern of "I and Thou, here and now."

Walter Lippmann was one of the first to see the impending fundamental changes when he wrote in 1914 in *Drift and Mastery:* "No mariner ever enters upon a more uncharted sea than does the average human being born in the twentieth century. Our ancestors thought they knew their way from birth to eternity; we are puzzled about the day after tomorrow." Today, one generation after these words were written, every value and tradition is under attack from some quarter. Yet, as Lippmann also pointed out, the overthrow of tradition and ancient laws, however outdated, will not bring a meaningful life, just as democracy does not automatically establish itself when a king is overthrown.

A Breakdown of Values

Traditions change slowly. Today, however, the breakdown is spreading so fast that it has opened the greatest value gap between generations in history. Many traditional cornerstones are crumbling: the sanctity of property, hereditary caste, the dogma of sin, blind obedience to authority, and even the value of tradition itself. People no longer accept mere age of an institution as reason for believing in it. Children do not trust their parents; citizens, their government; students, their professor; or churchgoers and even theologians, religious dogma. No citadel of tradition has remained intact.

When Frankl visited Japan, he spoke to his audiences about their high level of culture, their old traditions, and the rapid change in their cultural patterns—abolishing traditions within twenty years after having followed them for two thousand. In a question period a young girl stood up and asked, "How can we find meaning in this age of vanishing traditions and values?" The question made Frankl aware that he ought to stress the changing role of education.

For thousands of years the task of education was to pass values on from generation to generation. Today, Frankl argues, the mission of education is not merely to pass on knowledge but to help people refine their individual conscience so they become able to understand the meaning requirement of the specific moment. Further, he says, the crumbling of tradition affects only universal meanings, the values. Specific meanings cannot be affected by loss of tradition because they are not passed on but have to be found by each person for each specific situation. To discover these specific meanings we need a refined conscience and an ear trained to listen to its voice.

Austrian Jews experienced a sudden breakdown of values in 1938. All values collapsed: the government they had trusted, the society they had grown up in, the family that had protected them, and the laws that guaranteed their safety. Honesty turned out not to be the best policy, and it became necessary to lie in order to survive. Fathers did not know best and often lost their lives in following their own advice to wait quietly until things calmed down. The government did the murdering and stealing traditionally prohibited by law. The synagogues were burned down, and the churches, at best, were silent. The Cardinal of Vienna issued a proclamation supporting the godless regime. The Austrian Jews of 1938 found themselves in a moral wilderness with no signposts. What were the highest values? Survival? Courage? Honor? Cunning? Material advantages? They found no ends to strive for, only means; and the means ran wild. And then it dawned on them that in this wilderness they had nowhere to turn, that they were on their own.

The Refugee as a Guinea Pig

Since the traumatic experience of the refugee in 1938, the breakdown of traditional values has spread to the "settled" people in affluent societies. One might think of the refugees of the thirties as the guinea pigs in a gruesome experiment for everyone today: the experiment to find out how to survive and retain one's sense of meaning in the face of eroding values, fading traditions, and vanishing institutions; how to live in a world that denies values and traditions and at the same time makes it difficult for us to find meanings by disregarding our conscience. The greatest danger to our conscience is the continuing "reification," the transformation of human beings into things, because a thing has no conscience. It was Hitler's devilish scheme that he not only treated his victims as things but even succeeded, by pressure and propaganda, in convincing many, but never all, of his victims that they were things and had no recourse to their conscience. The same is done to us by the reductionism that treats us as mere animals or machines.

In a yet untranslated publication Frankl describes life in the concentration camp as the supreme degradation of human worth.[1] Imagine, he says, the state squeezing the last few drops of life out of human beings it has already condemned to death, forcing work out of them rather than killing them outright, feeding them only to get some use from them. "How often were we told in the concentration camps that we were not worth the soup fed to us—this soup which was our only warm meal and which we were to earn by digging ditches. We, the worthless ones, had to receive this unearned gift in proper gratitude: we had to take off our cap when we stood in line for it. Our life was no longer worth a bowl of soup, our death not worth a bullet—only a whiff of gas." This soup became no more than the oil necessary to keep a piece of machinery going a while longer. Human beings were things to be used as long as they were usable, to be discarded as efficiently and cheaply as possible when worn out. The same philosophy led to mass killings in mental institutions: the patient was considered a faulty piece of equipment and therefore useless.

The Hitler refugee in the thirties, trying to find a safe

spot to survive, was probably the closest to being a thing compared with any outside the concentration camp. And Hitler was able to make the world join him in considering the Jew a surplus commodity. At the Evian Conference Hitler offered the world forty thousand Jews for sale at $25,000 apiece, and some thirty nations rejected the offer. Individual nations made offers of their own, not based on what the refugees were (human beings) but on what they had (money, skills, and knowledge). Bolivia allowed a trickle of human merchandise across its borders if the immigrants were young and qualified farmers or investors with at least £1000; Haiti restricted immigration to those possessing $5000; Kenya narrowed its imports to those with £500; Paraguay admitted those with $1500 gold and the knowledge necessary for establishing new industries. Those who did not have what the market demanded found themselves dumped, often literally, into the ocean (on ramshackle boats that were not allowed to land anywhere) or burned (in concentration camps, like surplus coffee).

Becoming Things

In consequence, six million human beings perished, a monstrous toll. One might somehow accept this loss (even of parents, spouse, or friends) if one could see it as a sacrifice with some meaning behind it. Even the meaning of a warning: this is what happens when humans are treated as figures on transportation lists, as bookkeeping problems, as problems in efficient disposal. One can accept such mass misery—barely—as a warning that "it can happen here," in civilized countries, if for whatever reasons people are considered things. But the warning is not being heard. What Hitler did to his victims we now do to ourselves proudly and in the name of progress. We are well on our way to regarding ourselves as mere objects if governments become bureaucracies in which voters are merely statistics in a poll, if economists consider human beings as consumers to be brainwashed by advertisements, if management sees labor as tools to be replaced by more efficient machinery, if labor unions see their members as pawns in a bargaining process, if universities handle students like IBM cards and process them toward acquiring skills the market demands. Our reification happens in the namelessness of urban renewal that is building spiritual slums; in the graphs and charts in which human tragedy is presented; in the statistics of the unemployed, school dropouts, delinquents, crime casualties, and traffic accidents; in the projection of future wars in which casualties are calculated not in terms of six million victims but of sixty million, where killing is done not in personal confrontation but by pushbutton. If we become things, we have no tradition, only obsolescence, no value, only uses. As things among things, life is no longer meaningful. We have become means to an end.

Immanuel Kant warned that the human being must never be reduced to a means to an end. But, as Frankl wrote in 1958: "During past decades workers increasingly are being reduced to mere means. It is not work that is a means to an end, but the worker, the human being."[2] The situation has worsened in an era of automation, of mass advertisement that makes consumers a means for selling products, and of political cynicism that makes citizens a means for maneuvering votes. The more crowded the world becomes, the harder it is to pay attention to individuals, leading to regimentation in the name of orderliness. Regimentation makes people a means for the efficient functioning of economic and political machinery.

Groping for a Cure

Having diagnosed the ills of our times, Frankl tries to point the direction toward a cure. His cure—the return to the resources of our personal conscience—is neither unique nor new. What is novel is his challenge that education, in the broadest sense, must lead us back to the resources of our conscience and help us refine it. Although he sees conscience as the intuitive capacity to perceive the unique meaning *gestalt* of the unique life situation (*WM*, p. 19), he realizes that in the very young meaning must be channeled through the experiences of older people.

We cannot expect very small children to have a fully developed conscience, but neither do they possess the instincts of animals. They must be guided by experiences previous generations found useful. Early education must take the form of values handed down from the elders. But as children grow up, they become more and more able to take a stand that is independent of traditions and may even oppose traditions. But this may be the price we may have to pay for opposing societal values. What Frankl calls noögenic neuroses may be caused by a conflict between our true conscience and the mere superego (*PE*, p. 43).

The Danger of Mummification

It is the function of tradition to transmute knowledge into wisdom and pass it on to individuals who cannot possibly accumulate the wisdom of the ages by their own experiences. It is generally accepted that the child needs guidance, sometimes to the point of demanding blind obedience. Responsible parents will insist that their child obey certain rules with no questions asked: a child cannot afford to learn by trial and error the danger of walking into a fire or crossing a street against the traffic. Not every generation has the time and opportunity to find out for itself what is true and false, right and wrong, good and bad, desirable and undesirable. To have the guidance of childhood rules, rituals, commandments, and laws gives people security and direction. For this reason tradition, which passes on these rules, cannot be blindly disregarded. By discarding tradition indiscriminately, we are in danger of throwing out not only its outdated and objectionable trimmings but also time-tested truths.

Tradition is a blessing from the past and also a curse that threatens the future. Blind acceptance of tradition can be as dangerous as blind rejection because it mummifies values in a continually changing world. Today's fact is tomorrow's absurdity, and today's dream is tomorrow's reality. As we mature we check our traditional values against life's experiences, and they do not always fit. The same goes for maturing societies. Knowledge increases, and the wisdom based on this evolving knowledge must occasionally be brought up to date. Even encyclopedias become outdated and have to be revised. Most change is so gradual it is hardly noticed. Yet changes accumulate over centuries until the original laws and customs would not be recognized by their founders. The story is told in the Jewish Talmud (Menahot, 29 b) how Moses came down to earth and visited the school of the great scholar Rabbi Akiba, who taught many centuries later. Moses sat down in the last row and listened. But he did not recognize what the sage was teaching until Akiba closed his lecture with the words, "This is the law that Moses received on Sinai."

The greatest danger comes from those who insist they have found the truth once and for all. While the values passed on by tradition may open doors to age-old wisdom, they may also imprison if they are not constantly checked against the reality of growing knowledge. Nothing, neither a person nor a value, can be preserved by being locked up. A person will not stop aging in prison, and morals cannot be preserved when they are locked up in rules, laws, rituals, or holy books. Without constant change the most glorious tradition becomes a dead weight. Arturo Toscanini is said to have shouted to the musicians at rehearsals, "Routine—the death of music!" It is also the death of ethics, wisdom, and truth. Here is the basis for logotherapy's appeal, stressing the uniqueness of meaning over the universality of values.

Blindly accepted values are usually dangerous, but they are catastrophic in times of rapid changes. Occasionally, human knowledge comes in such rapid bursts that tradition is no reliable guide. We feel insecure, confused, and cannot find meanings by following outdated values. This may have happened in biblical times, when people in Babel built their tower of knowledge too high and fast and the result was chaos. In historical times periods of confusion occurred sporadically, for instance in the fifth pre-Christian century when scientific discoveries revolutionized the Greeks' picture of their world, their gods, and themselves. At the end of the medieval period a torrent of inventions and explorations radically changed people's outlook on the world they knew. And it is happening today. We are living through an era of unprecedented expansion of human knowledge.

From Meanings to Values

When traditions and established institutions are no longer trusted and universal values are breaking down, we are thrown back on our individual resources and have to find our own path to meaning. Logotherapy insists we can always find the specific meaning of a situation, even when universal traditional values have become useless.

Logotherapy also maintains that values can never disappear completely. Some can be cast off; others may change; but some universal values will remain because there are typical life situations we share with others. From this common ground values keep emerging. Even in times when traditional values become discredited and most people drift in a sea of apparent meaninglessness, some people with an alert conscience will recognize the unique meaning in the changed situation. New values will develop out of these individual findings of specific meanings. In Frankl's concept, the meanings of today become the values of tomorrow. The unique meaning found by unique individuals in response to specific situations may become a universal meaning, that is, a value (*WM*, p. 64).

Such a process may have occurred in Greece at the time of Socrates, in Palestine at the time of Jesus, and in India at the time of Buddha. Traditions fell apart, but the founders of religions discovered new meanings of their own, and set up new ideals to transmit.

If the present era is one of those turbulent intervals of transition, where are the new "prophets" who will show the way? The names of Gandhi, Schweitzer, Buber, and others have been mentioned. Perhaps the new prophet is wandering the earth, unknown, as Jesus was during the first thirty years of his life; perhaps he has not been born yet. Possibly the new message will come not through one messiah but through a multitude. Lewis Mumford, in his *Conduct of Life*, suggested that "security and salvation" might be achieved "if one person in ten were fully awakened, fully capable of exercising his higher centers of intelligence and morality." Mumford felt that in a democracy we cannot shift the burden of developing new values to individual messiahs and prophets. The burden has to be borne by us, by those of us whose conscience is refined enough to see unique meanings through the thicket of outdated universal values. Pointing the way to new meanings may require the same kind of sacrifices the religious prophets had to pay: ridicule, arrest, and perhaps death. But their views may prevail and show the way to a new morality.

The Role of Education

Frankl feels education can play a major part in guiding the young toward finding meaning. "It . . . stands to reason that in an age such as ours, that is to say, in an age of the existential vacuum, the foremost task of education, instead of being satisfied with transmitting traditions and knowledge, is to refine our capacity which allows man to find unique meanings. Today education cannot afford to proceed along the lines of tradition, but must elicit the ability to make independent and authentic decisions" (*WM*, p. 64).

This seemingly unorthodox goal of education is actually at least twenty-five hundred years old. It is the extension of Plato's concept that the purpose of education is the enlightenment of the ruler so that he might be the philosopher-king, the best informed, the most sensitive to the needs of the day, the person with the most responsive conscience. In a democracy, where everyone is the ruler, everyone needs to become so informed, sensitive, and responsive.

But in the most advanced democracies of the twentieth century we are just at the edge of such a concept. That is why it is education's task to help students discover today's values and find new priorities for old values—instead of simply passing on old value systems.

In a videotaped interview for the California College Association, Huston C. Smith asked Frankl how professors in universities can teach values to students and give them something like a meaning.[3] Frankl answered that "values cannot be taught; they must be lived. What we can give our students is not a meaning but an example, that is to say, the example of commitment to a cause worthy of such a commitment; for instance, science, truth, scientific research. This example we are giving will be watched and witnessed by our students." Smith then raised the question whether meanings and values can be carried to the students through the subject matter of the teachings. Frankl did not think so and added, "Today we must be satisfied that the selection of the subject matter does not undermine the basic meaning orientation of our youngsters." This is exactly what happens in the United States, when the human being is pictured in a reductionist manner. The original enthusiasm and idealism of our youth, their deep concern for values and ideals must not be weakened, for instance, by presenting values as "nothing but defense mechanisms or reaction formations." (Frankl often expresses his reaction to this kind of reductionism by saying he would not be willing to live for the sake of his reaction formation and even less willing to die for the sake of his defense mechanisms.) This view is supported by such university teachers as Nevitt Sanford of Stanford's psychology department, who stated that teachers cannot be effective unless they are prepared to deal with values and ideals and do not regard every moral stand a student takes as an expression of resistance, as a psychoanalyst would.[4]

Students are often taught that human existence can be explained only in terms of either the "machine model" or the "rat model" (to use a sarcastic phrase from Gordon W. Allport, a well-known critic of such models). Such a mechanistic kind of teaching is likely to undermine the students' belief in their freedom to make decisions. To what extent even high school students are being indoctrinated by such a deterministic approach is apparent in the experience of college advisors. They find that many entering freshmen, after being counseled, are happily surprised to hear that even at the ripe age of eighteen they may still alter the direction of their lives.

The new role of education is of concern to writers and educators both East and West. Krishnamurti maintains that only those who do not follow tradition can discover what is true; that we cannot leave the shelter of tradition and learn if we are afraid; and that the function of education is to eradicate this fear that destroys human thought, human relationship, and love. In the West, Robert Hutchins, former chancellor of the University of Chicago, sees education as a beacon rather than as a mirror of society—a restatement of Frankl's demand that education make the young a generation of "pacemakers" reaching for new goals rather than "peacemakers" adjusting to the old. Hutchins criticizes education's "service-station approach," which caters to the wishes of society, with all its mistaken goals, and treats society as a customer who is always right. The student is not educated, but trained to do what society wants and pays for. Hutchins defined American education as a system that fits young people into the existing environment, prepares them to adjust to the requirements of society and the job market, and trains them to accept rather than challenge values. "Students," he concluded on a note of optimism, "are looking for tasks and challenges; they do not want to fit into a society like automatons."[5]

Clarence Faust, president of the Fund for the Advancement of Education, criticized universities for merely confirming currently accepted opinions, ideologies, and prejudices. Walter Lippmann called on universities to accept their task to fill the spiritual and intellectual vacuum; and Rosemary Park, president of Barnard College, challenged college administrators to become "a kind of Socrates . . . asking the hurrying faculty what they mean by truth, justice, decency, even academic freedom. And we must ask the students . . . what they mean by integrity and how they recognize it, and, most important of all, what they think is going on." This, Ms. Park felt, "will begin the creation of a moral core, as Socrates' questions sought to clarify the will of Athens."[6]

New Values in Education

Nevitt Sanford pointed out that education must do more than emphasize values. It must stress the meanings behind values. Education stresses excellence, for instance, but excellence in what direction? Is it enough for a university to train specialists in their fields, scientists who will make brilliant discoveries without considering how they will be used? Universities can produce excellent physicists, chemists, and engineers; but unless they also produce conscientious human beings who care about people, the new knowledge will be misused. Sanford feels good teaching must include lessons on how to make individual decisions, and this capacity must be sharpened on controversial subjects (which many universities exclude). Professors must not only talk about controversial subjects but must get involved so students may see how they actually handle an issue. If the goal of education is a sharpening of individual conscience rather than training for socially acceptable careers, then, Sanford pointed out, today's primary and secondary education of the brightest children is inferior to that given to the less-bright ones. The parents of bright children want them to learn what will get them to college. They want facts poured into the children's heads, and the schools comply. The parents of less-bright children often are "content" to let the school concentrate on building character, developing judgment, helping the child to get the most out of life, and finding meanings and values.

Ironically, many of those "well-trained" students who have learned facts and skills may find that in this fast-changing world their skills have become obsolete by the time they are ready to start a career. But opportunities for which no formal education was available may present themselves. To take one striking example: John Glenn's teachers could not have given him a factual education enabling him to become an astronaut because such an occupation did not exist when he was getting his basic schooling. The catalogs of major universities list a number of fields practically unknown twenty years ago, such as exobiology (study of life beyond earth), bioengineering (engineering of artificial replacements of biological organs), cryogenics (study of how substances behave at extremely low temperatures), or bio-psychology (biological aspects of psychology). Yet educa-tion cannot be satisfied merely to train students in their special fields if they are to lead meaningful lives. To give students the feeling they are more than parts of a machine, they are part of evolving life, education must do more than train scientists to invent more gadgets; it must train them to respond more sensitively to the meanings of life and to help make society more responsible. At the same time edu-cation also must make all students familiar with what sci-ence is and what it can and cannot do, not because they may want to become scientists but because they want to be re-sponsible citizens in a world in which science has a big part.

It is difficult in the midst of the present transition period to foresee the new values that will emerge. However, lo-gotherapy is on firm ground with its demand for a strength-ening of personal conscience. Personal discovery helped people in previous in-between periods overcome the uncer-tainties caused by fading traditions. Socrates recommended personal discovery during his transition period. The unex-amined life, he said, is not worth living. Jesus, during an-other transition period, castigated the "hypocritical scribes and Pharisees" for merely following the letter of the law rather than trying to understand the meanings behind the laws. The Reformation, still another in-between era, shifted responsibility for personal conduct from the authority of church and pope to individual conscience. "Here I stand," Luther exclaimed. "God help me, I cannot do otherwise."

In all these instances people were confronted with a task: to know themselves, to see meanings behind the laws, to take a stand against dogma. It is doubtful if more than a few were ready to accept such freedom and responsibility in an-cient Greece, biblical Palestine, or medieval Europe. The question today is whether more than a few are ready now.

8. The Challenge of Freedom

Not yours to complete the work, neither are you free to reject it.

When Adam bit into that fateful piece of fruit, the human thirst for freedom was aroused and has never been quenched. We were free to choose between good and evil. Frankl, interpreting the expulsion from paradise as a loss of the comforting shackles of the instincts, sees us as free to find our own meanings and to develop our own values.

That this first freedom should manifest as disobedience to God will surprise no one who ever tasted the fruit of freedom in any form, for freedom always establishes itself as the decision to say no to authority. Children first taste freedom when they realize they can say no to their parents; slaves, when they become aware they can say no to their master; subjects, when they discover they can say no to their monarch. But it soon becomes clear that freedom is more than a breaking of chains. With emancipation the real tasks begin, because winning "freedom from"—namely, authority—is only the first step, followed by the necessity to decide on a "freedom to"—a commitment. Expressed in biblical terms, freedom to say no to God is followed by the necessity to eat one's bread by the sweat of one's brow. In logotherapeutic terms, freedom to lead a meaningful life is followed by the acceptance of responsibility. This was true of the biblical transition period between our animal stage of instincts and our human stage of freedom, and it is still true of the transition period of today.

Freedom in Theory and Practice

A fundamental difference exists, however, between the Garden of Eden and the present transition period. The former established human freedom on a precarious basis, one is tempted to say in theory only. Today freedom has been widely won in practice. Adam found out what children learn at an early stage: They have the capacity to disobey their parents, but parents have the capacity to punish. Who will blame our biblical ancestors for exercising their freedom in hesitation, fear, and trembling after Sodom and Gomorrah and the Flood? Who will blame our historical ancestors for cautiously feeling their way, threatened as they were by eternal hell fire or more immediately by death or torture decreed by a tyrant? Until modern times it required almost superhuman courage to stand up to the weight of institutional authority. In the land the king was absolute ruler; in the family the father was law; in school the schoolmaster was undisputed tyrant; and for the worker property owners and guild masters established rigid rules. In early science the researcher was ordered by church and state to follow a certain direction.

All this has changed. The struggle for freedom was joined in every field and has been won on all fronts. In the West, at least, we have emancipated ourselves from established church and civil authority. In a chain reaction of revolutions citizens have overthrown the absolute monarch; slaves and women have won emancipation; wives have achieved freedom from their husbands, children, from their fathers, pupils, from teachers, workers, from employers; and scientists are allowed the freedom of unhampered discovery. Our freedom is now a fact and at the same time life has lost its meaning. The struggle for freedom gives life content—goals to achieve. Once freedom from authority has been won, once independence and affluence has been achieved, the danger of the existential vacuum becomes real. For the second time we have eaten from the Tree of Knowledge and for the second time lost the shelter of the Garden of Eden. Again we are our own, but the consequence of expulsion in this affluent and automated society is not the curse of eating bread by the sweat of our brow but in boredom of spirit. And boredom is not the only consequence of our freedom. We also experience guilt because we know we could have chosen otherwise and anxiety because the burden of freedom is great. But freedom also brings joy because choosing is creative and meaning because creative activity provides reasons for meaning.

The Empty Canvas

One reason we feel unfulfilled today when we have achieved freedoms our ancestors only vaguely dreamed about is stated by Albert Camus. He names several of the traditional values whose loss turns our acts into empty, anxious gestures: music has lost melody; painting, form; poetry, rhyme and meter; thought, conviction; history, sense; and religion, God. In our surge toward unlimited freedom everything has become possible because everything is permitted, and the result is anxiety and emptiness.

A group of teenagers was discussing what was wrong with their parents, and one girl complained that hers were so permissive she had nothing to rebel against and so could not find what kind of person she was. Every youngster in that group had had similar experiences. An art professor at Sacramento State College observed that students often panic when confronting an empty canvas and are unable to paint. They experience the existential vacuum of the painter—no style is required, no tasks are demanded of them (as in former times when painters had patrons ordering portraits or the commemoration of important events, tasks now achieved efficiently by photography). After the shock of the empty canvas, the professor said, the students often go back to old masterpieces to find out what made them masterpieces, to search for significance.

Students panicking before the empty canvas because they have no rules to go by and are not asked to express anything but their private feelings are the prototype of many people today, free to do as they please. They panic. To hide their panic, they slavishly copy old masters or arbitrarily throw paint, even garbage, on the emptiness staring at them. But filling an empty canvas with just anything is no more meaning-fulfilling than copying traditional styles. In the present universal pursuit of freedom everyone can be a painter, poet, composer, philosopher, or moralist because anything goes. The old values are found wanting, so all values are thrown out. This is true in all fields of expression and inquiry. Artists express their own opinions unstifled by rules and conventions. Pragmatists present morals as expressions of personal feelings with no recourse to general guidelines. Sociologists and anthropologists stress the diversity of morals and refuse to make value judgments. Semanticists express doubt that we can understand another person's language. Psychologists point to the unconscious as a reason we cannot even understand ourselves. We have placed our faith in science, but science too turns out to be less than an absolute master with a reliable set of rules. Science is no longer considered a source of complete truth but rather a system of hypotheses that change as new knowledge is acquired. Probability has replaced certainty in statistics, and physics has admitted its uncertainty principle. If physics has its uncertainty principle, what can be said about the certainty of morals?

Herein lies the danger—that, using our newly gained freedom, we will arbitrarily develop personal standards: our own rules in the arts, our own hypotheses in science, our own language, morality, beliefs, and meanings. In our lunge toward freedom we have gone on a rampage of do-it-yourself rules. If this tendency continues and we all become master builders of our own values, the world will become a Babel of confusion; and our diversified, self-made morality may well lead to destruction. God's promise to Noah never again to unleash another flood does not preclude the possibility that we ourselves unlock the floodgates. Human freedom, running wild, allows us to say no even to our own existence.

The Positive Value of Freedom

Logotherapy proclaims freedom as an exclusively human quality that allows us to rise above all biological, psychological, and environmental limitations. But Frankl also warns that "freedom will degenerate into arbitrariness unless it is lived in terms of responsibleness" (*WM*, p. 49). As long as we regard freedom as something merely negative, as a "freedom from," as license to do as we please, it leads to boredom and frustration. Freedom is not "doing what we want" but "wanting what is demanded." We are free if we see ourselves as part of an order and response-able to it. We are unfree if we reject any order. True freedom is consent to productive activity, a free decision for someone or something, performing a self-chosen task. Only then is freedom a positive value, a "freedom to." Freedom not used responsibly only widens the existential vacuum.

A glance at how freedoms recently acquired are being used shows this danger indeed exists. Many freedoms, gained with effort and sacrifice, are being used arbitrarily and lead to negative values. Students fighting for freedom of expression on the campus use it to voice not only beliefs but obscenities—and they feel restless and frustrated. Workers have gained freedom from feudal working conditions but also the freedom to paralyze industry and the public—and have lost their traditional pride in workmanship. Emancipated women have achieved economic and sexual equality, may send their children to nurseries, and can divorce their husbands—and are restless and dissatisfied. Teenagers are using their freedom from parental authority to defy authority and participate in violence and sex orgies—and have lost the security of being an integral and useful part of the family. The freedoms guaranteed in the Bill of Rights, exercised without self-restraint, have led to murder ("the right to bear arms"), pornography and filibuster ("freedom of speech"), riots ("freedom of assembly"), and the election of incompetent, corrupt, or demagogic politicians.

The danger of missing the positive value of freedom can be illustrated by our conquest of poverty. Although, deplorably, thirty-three million of our two hundred million Americans are still classified as "poor," for the first time in history the poor are a minority. The majority in Western countries have achieved freedom from want. How will they use this freedom? Will they go on a rampage in jubilation at having succeeded in overthrowing the tyranny of poverty? Will they celebrate "freedom from" like children going through piles of Christmas presents, unwrapping them in a hurry, playing with them for a while, and then, bored, throwing them on the national junk pile? Or will the "haves" of the earth widen their horizon and use their freedom from want in response to the needs of the "have nots"? After World War II, at the dawn of this era of plenty, the idea of helping others was ridiculed as "giving milk to the Hottentots." Since then, American leaders have acknowledged their responsibleness through the Marshall Plan, the Peace Corps, and the Poverty Program. Will individuals, in their own lives, accept similar commitments? It is perhaps too much to expect that human beings, after a million years of scarcity, should respond to the sudden outpouring from the horn of plenty with anything but grabbing and with predictable consequences—the existential vacuum. John Steinbeck, in a *Saturday Evening Post* article, "What Happened to America?" said, "I strongly suspect that our moral and spiritual disintegration grows out of our lack of experience with plenty." We have developed an economy and a technology that enable the majority, not just an aristocratic elite, to live in plenty. Unaccustomed to abundance, the majority, not just an elite, lives in boredom, frustration, and emptiness.

The Freedom Leisure Brings

The new experience with plenty extends to the abundance of time we now have on our hands. Leisure was once the prerogative of the aristocrats, and they usually frittered it away in boredom. For the majority of a nation to have excess time is something new, and we have not yet learned how to use it. We are in somewhat the same position as our grandparents, who built the first motor car in the shape of a horseless carriage because that was the shape they were used to. We are trying to build our first model of abundant leisure in the shape of the traditional Sabbath—a day on which we have the oppportunity, in fact the obligation, to be idle. God made the world in six days and rested on the seventh. That was our model. The Protestant ethic considered idleness a sin during the first six days and work a sin on the seventh. The church and civil authorities codified that concept. So ingrained is this concept of leisure that some people still feel guilty reading fiction during the week because they consider it sinful to read books that are merely entertaining during working hours.

We are only beginning to realize what leisure can mean. Automation releases masses of workers every week; and before today's youth reach middle age, work may consume twenty hours and leisure one hundred hours a week. But modern technology brings about changes that go far beyond technical matters. It makes work, which used to be a commitment, a mere job. Few people can honestly say it would make much difference if they were replaced in their jobs by someone else or even by a machine. This was not true of the artisan, the medieval workman, or the growing child helping mother in the home or father on the farm. Even the slave in a pre–Civil War home was more personally needed than most employees are today. Technology makes us feel superfluous in work and makes work in many cases meaningless. But it also frees us from meaningless work and gives us leisure for tasks that can make life meaningful.

To realize the opportunities of this gift, we will have to reverse our ideas about leisure. As long as six days a week were needed to do the work necessary for survival, the seventh day was important for contemplation and spiritual refreshment. As an unintentional side effect, religion was concentrated for most people on Sunday only. Now, with six days of work no longer needed for survival, we can streamline the leisure model. No longer do we have to find meaning in work for six days and in contemplation on the seventh. We can spread meaningful activities to our leisure hours and meaningful experiences to our working days. Leisure is not merely absence of work or freedom merely absence of tyranny. The vacuum of nonwork can be given content; the vacuum of meaningless work can be filled. As we enter the era of plenty of time, we suspect that eternal leisure is not the definition of heaven but of hell. We realize that the existential vacuum cannot be filled with idleness or with activity for activity's sake.

Frankl speaks of "Sunday neurosis," which drives more people to suicide on their days off than on work days, even when humdrum jobs fills their existence. The idleness of retirement can be deadly for those who do not fill their newly won freedom with some task. Passive watching, such as television, can be a meaningful experience if you select programs; indiscriminate watching only deepens the existential vacuum. Movie actress Anne Baxter, who may have learned to think independently from her grandfather, Frank Lloyd Wright, speculated that the unrest of bored young people may be caused by their treating life as if it were a continuation of television: They just sit back and let life pass by, without participating.

Activity for activity's sake is equally useless. Young people especially want to be "where the action is." Many gain the illusion of activity through speed. They get into their cars and drive, fast and aimlessly. The feverish desire to be active has also affected the wealthy and successful, so much so that Frankl speaks of the "executive disease," characterized by hypertension and an inclination to coronaries. In a seminar for policy-making executives in California, Frankl gave a "case history" of an executive disease. A young Italian industrialist came to him with a depression. Physically, he was well. During the course of the examination Frankl probed him for some unfulfilled desires. The patient told him that he owned a private plane, but this did not satisfy him. He was therefore driving himself with overtime work so he could afford a jet. "This patient," Frankl told his audience of executives, and his tongue was not too much in cheek, "was suffering most typically from executive disease: He was trying to run away from his inner void to the extent that only jet-propelled speed could help him escape."[1]

The Private Desert

There is nothing wrong with speed. To put the blame for our psychological ills on the tempo of our times, Frankl declares, "is a trivial and incorrect diagnosis. Speed may cause physical illnesses and death but, psychologically speaking, our desire for speed is not a cause of illness but rather a misguided attempt to rid ourselves of our feeling of emptiness. We are trying to run away from it, and the faster the better." He quotes a Viennese comedian who sings a little ditty, sitting on his motorcycle. Each stanza ends with the words, "I have no idea where I'm going, but I don't mind as long as I'm getting there fast" (*WM*, p. 97).

Speeding is, to use Frankl's term, a "centrifugal" leisure activity, an attempt to escape from ourselves, an aimless flying off in all directions. He pleads for "centripetal" leisure activities, directed toward, not away from, our center, allowing us to confront ourselves and our existential problems. He recommends "a private desert" for everyone, some place where we can retreat to think about ourselves—a room, a patch of grass, a cottage in the woods, or a beach. My wife and I have accompanied the Frankls to their own private desert, the Rax Mountains in the Alps. He speeds there in his car as fast as he can in order to spend hours walking and rock climbing in lonely contemplation or in the company of fellow climbers.

Most people evade such confrontations with themselves; they plunge into meaningless activities to run away from their existential problems. During the day, Frankl says, their thoughts are constantly interrupted by phone calls, secretaries, social obligations, children, and the noises of leisure—hi-fi, television, radio, and stereo. Then at night they are plagued by "existential sleeplessness"; the unfinished thoughts do not let them fall asleep. But instead of taking this opportunity to think through their problems, they take sleeping pills. They fall asleep but also fall prey to the repression of their existential problems. They do not have the courage to be lonely, to face and solve their existential questions (*PE*, p. 41).

Responsibility and Responsibleness

The Sunday neurosis, the executive disease, and the other symptoms of the existential vacuum can be prevented by responding to challenges and tasks. Dr. Harvey Cushing, at the age of eighty-two, told a friend, "The only way to endure life is always to have a task to complete." The validity of this "prescription" has been attested to by American army and navy psychiatrists, even in extreme situations such as in North Korean and Vietnamese prisoner-of-war camps and German death camps.

Our freedom of choice, even in prisons, may lead to either a meaningful or an empty life. To be meaningful, as stated before, life must be lived freely and responsibly. The Garden of Eden was a place of blind and instinctual obedience to the creator, with no tasks or challenges. It was a garden of nonfreedom and nonresponsibility. When Adam ate the fruit, he found himself free to know good and evil, responsible for living in freedom, outside the protection of paradise. He became the only animal that could reach out for the good but also suffer from such evils as inadequacy, discontent, unhappiness, and boredom. To avoid the negative aspects of humanness, we must accept responsibleness in the three areas where meaning is available. As Frankl puts it, we are responsible for "what we do, whom we love, and how we suffer."[2]

If responsibility is the cure for meaninglessness, why do we suffer more today from meaninglessness than ever before? Are we less responsible than Vikings, Crusaders, or Huns? The answer lies in logotherapy's distinction between responsibility and responsibleness. Responsibility is imposed from the outside; responsibleness is freely chosen. Our ancestors were given responsibilities by some authority. Responsibility within the family was clearcut—the man was the breadwinner; the woman, the homemaker; and the children the helpmates. The church laid down responsibility for parishioners in their tightly knit parishes, providing security in ritual and sacraments from birth to death. The guilds demanded training and craftsmanship from their members; the schools insisted on learning and discipline from students. In a society where responsibility was given and unquestioningly accepted, life had content. Today we have freed ourselves from most outside authority; but where responsibility is not accepted from an authority, responsibleness must come from within. Responsibleness means inner discipline. We respond not because we are forced to but because we so decide. Traditional authorities, such as priest, king, father, or teacher, may impose responsibilities but not responsibleness because responsibleness results from our own decision. Responsibility without freedom is tyranny. Freedom without responsibleness is arbitrariness, leading to boredom, emptiness, anxiety, and neurosis.

Two incidents in Frankl's life illustrate the intricate relationships among freedom, responsibility, responsibleness, and the existential vacuum. When he lectured to a group of American psychiatrists, one of them commented that he had just returned from Moscow, where he had found a lower incidence of neurotic illnesses. He thought the finding supported the conclusions of logotherapy because the people behind the Iron Curtain were confronted by their governments with immediate tasks they were forced to complete. Two years later Frankl told an assembly of the Psychiatric Association of Krakow, Poland, what the American psychiatrist had said—that in Communist countries people are confronted with tasks and therefore are less neurotic than Americans. When he saw several smiles in the audience, he added "You are less neurotic than the Americans because you have more tasks to complete, but don't forget that the

Americans have retained the freedom also to choose their tasks, a freedom which sometimes seems denied to you" (*WM*, p. 48). How wonderful a world it would be, he concluded, to have meaningful tasks to fulfill and also the freedom to choose them according to one's own conscience.

Authority from Within

Thus "freedom from" rejects outside authority but "freedom to" requires a self-imposed authority from within. Today we are in a crucial in-between period. We no longer accept meanings as dictated by church, state, family, and the other traditional institutions; and we are unprepared to direct our own lives. Responsibility from above is rejected and responsibleness from within is not yet widely accepted. Thus we feel abandoned, unprotected, drifting, uprooted, and despairing.

Ours may be the most difficult transition period to overcome, but overcome we must because the consequence of failure is more severe than ever before. To borrow a phrase from the civil rights movement, in the slogan "We shall overcome" each of the three words is significant. We have the freedom to *overcome* the difficulties of the transition period. It is *we* who have to do the overcoming; we cannot rely on anyone else to do it for us. And we *shall* overcome, not right away, but in the future; we need patience, determination, and will. The pursuit of meaning is the prescribed course.

Standing in the midst of this crucial interim period, we cannot know where our newly won freedoms will lead. We know where excess freedom often led the aristocrats. They ritualized their behavior, dress, speech, games, the right season in which to do things, and became slaves to these rituals. They also engaged in less harmless activities to keep busy. They made war, slaughtered animals for fun, and risked their fortunes at gambling and their lives in duels. Rarely were they ready to accept inner discipline when outer authority was gone. Will the masses do better? The danger, in Frankl's words, is apparent: "Unlike other animals, man is not told by drives and instincts what he must do, and unlike man in former times, he is no longer told by tradition and traditional values what he should do. Now, lacking these directives, he sometimes does not know what he wants to do. The result? Either he does what other people do—which is conformism—or he does what other people want him to do which is totalitarianism" (*UC*, p. 25).

In either case the freedom won in the American and French revolutions will be in danger, for the great aims of these revolutions are lost when we succumb to dictators but also when we surrender to conformity. A society to which one conforms does not promote freedom, only equality. Personal liberty, Frankl says, is sacrificed for an impersonal equality; and fraternity degenerates into a mere herd instinct.

But loss of freedom threatens from yet another direction. After rejecting predetermination on religious grounds, we accept it on scientific grounds. We feel determined by our genes, glands, drives, emotions, early childhood experiences, environment, economic conditions, and god of science only knows what else. Logotherapy asserts that in spite of these scientifically established limitations we retain a core area of freedom no one except we ourselves can take from us, by not using it. Logotherapy encourages us to use our freedom and use it responsibly lest, like the sorcerer's apprentice, we become slaves to our own scientific creation.

Search for New Values

We must, as in the past, emerge from the present transition period with a newly adjusted set of values, but perhaps with a difference. In previous interim periods value revolutions started in the minds of individuals. This time it could be a collective effort.

The present value revolution started with the young. It is youth that suffers most from the existential vacuum, not because they are sick but because they are searching for meaning and cannot find it through tradition. In the sixties they were mostly *against*, not knowing what they were *for*. Or, as Frankl punned, they were not really "protesting" but rather "antitesting." They had no particular ideology, they were against capitalism, communism, colonialism, patriarchism, patriotism, and a moralism they considered "phony." They wanted to act but were not sure in which direction. They did not want merely to study history; they wanted to make it. They did not want to learn about old social orders; they wanted to topple them. They protested—against the war in Vietnam, sexual taboos, conformity in clothing, puritanical parents, and windbag orators. They wanted to "find themselves"; they wanted to find direction in a sea of chaos, but not along traditional guidelines.

Theirs was a new kind of revolt. Past revolutions were fought against political and economic exploitation, as they are still fought in many parts of the world. In the West these revolutions are largely won. The revolutions in the West are waged against affluent and nonoppressive societies. We see a revolt of the young "haves," who have an abundance of material goods but do not want to pay their elders' price of compromise and the double standards the young see as the consequence of outdated values. It is a revolution in search for meaning.

The sixties brought the double standard into focus. The young rebelled against a society that spent billions to pulverize a few hamlets on the other side of the globe while American cities became slums. They rebelled against a value priority that financed space travel while in their own country transporation became antiquated and dangerous. They rebelled against a system that trained healthy eighteen-year-olds to kill while maintaining laws against taking the life of an unborn embryo doctors feel may be deformed.

The young of the sixties did not automatically assume that a gentlemen's agreement was made by gentlemen, that the white man's burden is a burden for the white man, or that national honor is honorable under all circumstances. They rejected such cornerstones of conventional society as civil obedience, the accumulation of wealth, the sanctity of marriage, Christianity, and "my country right or wrong" patriotism. They denounced a society that imprisoned the young for smoking marijuana while their parents were hooked on a cafeteria of pills; a hedonistic, prestige-conscious, materialistic society that "brainwashed a generation of kids into a revolving charge account and buying junk" and "screwed up the land and the water and the air for profit."[3]

As we entered the seventies, a shift toward the positive was noticeable. The reaction to Vietnam was essentially negative, rebellion *against* this particular war, authority, and the dogma of monolithic communism. The reaction to Watergate had positive aspects, people demanded ethics in government. They elected a president not because he was especially qualified but because he was perceived as truly moral. Through the tax revolt they demanded frugality in government. The American dogma that "bigger is better" was challenged with "small is beautiful." The positive aspects of the new direction most clearly emerge from the ecological movement. Ecologists fight the values of the establishment in order to maintain clean air and water for themselves and for future generations who would suffer the consequences of our pollution and appetite for energy. They supplement our freedom to "be fertile and multiply, to fill the earth and subdue it" with the responsibleness in self-imposed restrictions.

In a way this trend constitutes a return to old values: frugality, morality, and responsibility. What is new is that these values are not decreed from above but chosen from within. The difference became clear to me in a seminar I gave at the University of California. During it Frankl spoke in the area and the class went to hear him. At the next session the class was divided. Some were enthusiastic, others, disappointed. They said things like, "He is trying to sneak the old morality in by the back door" or "Whenever I hear someone talk about tasks and responsibility, it turns me off." During the subsequent discussion one of the older students asked one of the "rebels": "But you said yourself that your years in the Peace Corps were most satisfying. Wasn't that a task?" "Oh, yes," was the answer, "but it was a task I had selected for myself!" He stopped and realized the difference between tasks that are ordered and those that are self-chosen commitments, the difference between responsibility and responsibleness. Of course, only the latter is logotherapeutically relevant.

Fewer and fewer people find meaning in tasks that are commanded; more and more realize that a taskless life is empty, that they have to replace ordered tasks with self-chosen ones. We are free to reject any duty we find meaningless but we have to replace it with a meaningful commitment. Freedom gives us the license to be immoral but also the opportunity to achieve true morality based on our *decision* to be moral. We are no longer motivated to be moral by fear of hell fire, witch hunts, tarring and feathering, or the parental rod. Only a generation ago a young man may have been celibate because he was afraid of venereal diseases and a young girl, because she was afraid of pregnancy. Now, in the age of antibiotics and the pill, if young people abstain from sexual activity before marriage, it is because they choose to do so.

This does not mean the young have become a "moral" generation. Far from it. Many are acutely suffering from an existential vacuum they desperately are trying to fill with drugs, alcohol, rebellion, and violence. We still live in the chaos of a transition period. But the pendulum is swinging back from the unlimited permissiveness of the sixties, when parents and teachers were afraid to make demands on children, when the goal of the good life was "doing your own thing," and when it was considered healthy to vent anger and hate without restrictions. College students, their freedoms won, are using them in increasing numbers to study in the classes of their choice. Women and racial minorities, having made at least some progress in their fight for equality, prepare themselves for jobs in which they wish to prove themselves equal. The violence of the Black Panthers of the sixties has made room for leaders who preach responsibleness and self-reliance.

These new leaders realize that freedom will come when we are willing to restrain our personal freedom for the sake of a totality of which we are a part and justice will come when those who are not hurt by injustice are as indignant as those who are. Too long were we told what we "ought" to do; now we have the freedom to do what we think is right without direction from institutions still geared to the values of yesteryear. But directions we must have, and these come from our own choice. As Frankl says, "freedom is transformed into responsibleness." In his American lectures he often suggests that we "supplement the Statue of Liberty on your East Coast by a Statue of Responsibleness on your West Coast" (*WM*, p. 49). One might add, the torch that directs the "poor (and) . . . huddled masses" toward freedom must be reinforced by an inner light that directs them toward a meaningful use of liberty—or the land of the free may become a land of the frustrated.

9. Applications of Logotherapy

People tell me I oversimplify.... They overcomplicate.

ERIC BERNE

Because the search for meaning is frustrated in our materialistic, hedonistic, reductionistic, alienating, and complex society, a meaning-oriented therapy is needed to help us listen to "the unheard cry for meaning," to use the title of one of Frankl's books. Logotherapy does not claim to be a cure-all or the only school of therapy trying to find answers to mental discomfort. It moves in a definite direction, however—away from adjustment, toward individual responsibility. It sees us not determined by drives but oriented toward meaning. It emphasizes mental health rather than mental disease, the total person rather than the psychophysical only, freedom more than limitations, challenge of the future rather than past traumas. It helps to build strength, to cope with the stresses of modern life.

Logotherapy operates on philosophical as well as medical levels. No therapy can function without its own views about human nature. Freud, a medical doctor, set out to find cures for diseases of the mind. One generation after his death his view of human nature has revolutionized not only medicine but practically all aspects of human life—education, child rearing, marital relationships, politics, law, writing and literary criticism, sales techniques, work, and leisure. Freud's philosophy in each of these areas had greater impact than his therapy had on mental health. More people were prompted to buy goods, elect political candidates, or write and read books through applications of Freudian discoveries about human nature than have been cured by psychoanalysis. Freud's contribution to the understanding of our behavior and our relationships with others is spectacular. His contribution to curing the sick is less striking when compared with medical advances in other fields during the same period, for example, antibiotics or new surgical techniques. Psychoanalysis has been most influential in nonmedical areas, and its success is mostly the result of its philosophy. Through Freud's influence we have become aware of inner forces that motivate our actions, feelings, and thoughts; and this awareness helps in retaining and recovering our mental health.

Other schools of therapy have refined self-understanding by drawing attention to such areas as will to power and the influence of society. These therapies contribute to mental health at least as much through their philosophies as through medical techniques. This is also true of logotherapy. The foregoing eight chapters have presented logophilosophy. It helps us avoid existential despair by guiding us toward meaning and thus is preventive and indirect therapy. This chapter presents ways logophilosophy can be used in curative and direct therapy.

Philosophy as Therapy

Logophilosophy contributes to mental well-being through its interpretation of personal existence, but it is not the therapist who is the interpreter. Frankl conceives the role of the therapist not as that of a painter who presents "the world as he sees it" but as that of an eye specialist who helps patients "see the world as it is."

The centerpiece of your "world as it is" is self-knowledge—*you* as you are. This statement has to be taken with two grains of salt: First, there is no such person as you "as you are," only "as you are becoming." Second, you are the centerpiece only in the sense that your self-centeredness includes others. Meaning will come through constant striving toward a new self that is closer to your potentials than your present self and through constant attempts to interrelate with others. Logophilosophy's advice is know yourself as an indivisible entity of body, psyche, and spirit; do not allow yourself to be reduced below that totality.

Seeing ourselves as we are, we admit there is truth in biology's claim that our brain is a form of computer; we accept as truth the claim of psychoanalysis that we are a battleground of psychological forces and sociology's claim that we are the outcome of our environment. But we are also infinitely more. The damage, warns Frankl, comes from believing we are *nothing but* a computer, a battleground, and an outcome, from disregarding the human dimension and projecting everything onto the psychophysical plane. Frankl defines reductionism as a new kind of nihilism—a belief not in nothingness but in "nothingbutness."

Logophilosophy becomes therapeutic when it strengthens our belief that we can, for example, experience genuine love—not merely a reaction formation concealing hostility or "nothing but" a sublimation of sex—or that we possess a genuine conscience—not merely the result of parental punishment. Logophilosophy proclaims that love, conscience, art, religion, and desire for truth and meaning are authentic phenomena and not just sublimations, repressions, and defense mechanisms. Logophilosophy protects us against the reductionism promoted by popular books, articles, movies, and even analysts of the orthodox school. The New York psychiatrist Lawrence J. Hatterer observed that "many an artist has left the psychiatrist's office enraged by interpretations that he writes because he is an injustice collector or a sadomasochist; that he acts because he is an exhibitionist;

that he dances because he wants to seduce his audience sexually; or that he paints to overcome strict bowel training by free smearing."[1]

Where this kind of reductionism can lead is indicated by California sociologist William Irwin Thompson, who wrote in *Main Currents in Modern Thought:* "If the most educated members of our culture continue to look at geniuses as disguised sexual perverts, if they think that all values are ... specious fiction ... how can we be alarmed if the mass of our culture shows little regard for values and instead loses itself in itself in an orgy of consumption, crime, and immorality."[2] Logophilosophy liberates us from the shackles of reductionism, dehumanization, depersonalization, and reification. It restores full human capacities and thus health to people who believed they were sick because they were frustrated.

How patients see themselves and their basic nature creates a lasting feedback. If they interpret themselves in mechanical terms, their attention is directed toward manipulation. If they interpret human nature analytically, their attention is focused on living out their drives and needs. If they interpret human nature logotherapeutically, they become aware of tasks, values, goals and responsibleness. Logotherapy is education but it is "autogenous education," that is, patients learn to educate themselves.

The Four Steps of Therapy

As mentioned before, the noëtic dimension cannot become sick but sickness can originate there, in which case Frankl speaks of noögenic neuroses. The symptoms of such neuroses may be physical sickness, psychological disorders such as depression, or existential frustration and despair. The logotherapeutic treatment of neuroses usually consists of four steps based on Frankl's original discoveries and sharpened by the clinical experiences of Elisabeth Lukas, logotherapist and head of a counseling center in Munich.

The first goal of the logotherapist is to help patients separate themselves from their symptoms. The resources of their noëtic dimension are tapped, the defiant power of their spirit is aroused, making them aware that they are not identical with their fears, obsessions, inferiority complexes, depressions, and emotional outbursts. They see they are not helpless victims of their biological, psychological, or sociological fate; do not have to remain the way they are; and can take a stand in any situation. The logotherapist removes the structures of dependency patients have built up in their attempt to explain the symptoms to themselves and that, through negative feedback, drive them ever more deeply into their conviction that these symptoms are inescapable traps.

The methods by which the therapist helps patients gain distance from their symptoms differ from case to case. Mere persuasion, however, will not work. The more one tries to persuade patients that, for instance, things are not all that bad or that they "should" do this or that, the more their resistance is aroused, resulting in a "yes, but" reaction. The therapist does better to use the methods logotherapy has developed for its own purposes, which are discussed later in this chapter. It is also possible to adapt these methods or develop new ones, following the general principles of logophilosophy. The patients begin to see what they unconsciously already know: they are, first and foremost, human beings with a capacity to find meaning. Only secondarily are they individuals with certain shortcomings, which they can overcome, and certain unwanted patterns, which they can break.

The second step aims at a modification of attitudes. Once patients have gained distance from their symptoms, they are open to new attitudes toward themselves and their lives.

One woman was unable to establish satisfactory relationships with men; in fact, she could not form any close friendships with anybody and led a lonely and embittered life.
Her symptom was loneliness, and the explanation she had
formulated for herself was, "My mother never loved me,
therefore I am unable to love." Under the guidance of the
therapist she reviewed her life and remembered instances
where she had been able to love. It was always she who had
fled the encounter, and not because of some inescapable
pattern that went back to her childhood. She realized she
had choices and in a reversal of attitudes decided, "My
mother never loved me, and I know how it feels. I'll therefore make a special effort not to spread this feeling of un-
lovingness any further." Nothing had changed except her
attitude. With the therapist's encouragement she selected
the first step on her new path. She befriended a little girl
whose father had deserted his family and whose mother
made no secret that the child was a burden.

The new attitude is not forced upon patients, but the
therapist must watch for telltale signs from the patients' unconscious indicating the direction they might want to
change. Once a "logo-hook" emerges, the therapist is justified in supporting the decision with all the resources of logotherapy. If the new attitude runs into a dead end, the patient has at least learned other choices are possible and can
try another direction.

Only in emergencies, such as threatening suicide, is the
therapist justified in suggesting new attitudes. In such cases,
which Frankl calls "last aid," there is no time to lead the patient to gain distance from his or her symptoms; and the
therapist will try to tip the scale toward life and meaning by
his or her own argument. Even in these cases the argument
must remain within the value system of the patient, not of
the therapist.

After a successful modulation of attitudes, the third step

in the logotherapeutic treatment usually takes care of itself: The symptom disappears or becomes manageable. Where depression is caused by circumstances beyond control, the new attitude helps patients accept their fate so they are able to bear it. The logotherapist cannot restore an amputated leg but can help the amputee live with one leg without succumbing to apathy or despair and without revolting against fate in frustration.

When the third step, the reduction of symptoms, has been successful, patients experience such a positive feedback from their new attitudes that they are open to an orientation toward meaning. The fourth and final step in logotherapy, then, is prophylaxis, to secure the patient's mental health for the future. Patients are guided toward meaning. All meaning potentials of their lives and their particular situation are discussed, enriched, and extended. The value hierarchy is clarified so they are protected from future existential frustrations. They are led to assume responsibility.

Logotherapeutic Methods

Because logotherapy stresses the specifically human dimension, its methods appeal to the patients' human qualities, such as self-discovery, choice making, responsibleness, and self-transcendence. Excluded are methods that are manipulative, reductionistic, or dehumanizing.

Because logotherapy stresses uniqueness, improvisation plays an important role. Once an atmosphere of trust has been established, any method that is compatible with logophilosophy can be tried. List making is used to make patients aware of choices. Painting, fantasizing, or interpreting dreams help patients see repressed meanings, ignored goals, and unconscious value preferences. Psychodramas can become logodramas by giving participants a chance to act out parts of the self they still want to become. Among the methods Frankl developed are the Socratic dialogue, paradoxical intention, and dereflection.

Socratic Dialogue

The Socratic dialogue, or self-discovery discourse, enables patients to get in touch with their noëtic unconscious and become aware of their true evaluation of themselves and their potentials, their preferred directions, and their deepest meaning orientation. From childhood on they have put on masks in order to please, to be accepted, and to avoid guilt. The self-discovery discourse helps patients discover their selves under the masks—the beautiful selves that can be actualized toward meaning and the ugly selves that can be improved or at least honestly accepted.

The Socratic dialogue takes its name from the Socratic concept of the teacher. The teacher's job was not to pour information into students but to make students conscious of what they already knew deep within. Socrates saw the teacher as a midwife helping students give birth to their unconscious knowledge. The logotherapist, too, is a midwife—or midhusband, as the case may be—to help patients give birth to their unconscious goals.

In the Socratic dialogue the therapist poses questions in such a way that patients become aware of their unconscious decisions, their repressed hopes, and their unadmitted self-knowledge. The dialogue explores experiences of the past and fantasies for the future, revives overlooked peak experiences, reevaluates situations that had appeared meaningless, and draws attention to disregarded achievements. The dialogue is a useful tool in all four steps of logotherapy. It helps patients gain distance from their symptoms, guides them toward new attitudes, draws attention to the achievement of having conquered their symptoms, and enables therapist and client to go on a common search for meaning.

In this common search the logotherapist is a participating

partner. He or she does not accept explanations of "hopeless situations," although the facts may seem to warrant the complaint. The logotherapist insists that choices are always available, if only choices of attitudes. Merely understanding patients' feelings and mirroring their difficulties is not enough because this only pushes them deeper into their problems. Instead the logotherapist challenges the patients to make choices, accept responsibilities and commitments, and take steps—be they ever so small—in a new direction, away from the problem.

This challenging is done with empathy. The encounter between patient and therapist (or among group partici-pants) never becomes hostile and negative; logotherapist and patient are allies in their common search for a way out of frustration and emptiness. Nevertheless the logotherapist must be able to say "No" or "Stop, that far and no farther!" Therapists must say no to patients who feel completely de-termined by uncontrollable factors. They must be able to say to an obsessive-compulsive: "No, you won't do what you are afraid of doing; your very fear protects you." They must be able to say to a depressed person: "No, it isn't true that your life has lost its purpose. You are wrong, and I can prove it to you."

The Socratic dialogue may start out with a struggle be-tween patient and therapist, but it becomes a common struggle in the search for meaning. The struggle is over when the patient becomes independent. Elisabeth Lukas, the director of a counseling center in Munich, Germany, concludes, "When the patient has found his self, the thera-pist must quietly step back, he has nothing more to add. In this common struggle, the patient must give his trust, but the therapist must give everything he is capable of. For this is the demand for the logotherapist: It is not enough to be a good psychologist, not even to be a good psychotherapist. The therapists in their work must also act as human beings.

They have to watch that their patients, during their counseling sessions, are never reduced to anything less than humans."[3]

Logotherapy has been given credit for "rehumanizing" psychotherapy, and the Socratic dialogue is its main vehicle for the rehumanization. Abraham Maslow, in *Religion, Values, and Peak Experiences*, points to the I-Thou encounter between existential therapist and patient that the mirror-type analyst cannot achieve. "Even the classical psychoanalysts would now be willing to admit," Maslow says, "that care, concern, and agapean love for the patient are implied by the analyst in order that therapy may take place." But even this therapist-patient encounter on the human level is not enough. Logotherapy, says Frankl in *Psychotherapy and Existentialism*, goes a step further and opens that two-sided relationship to include a third "partner"—meaning. The Socratic dialogue is an I-Thou relationship between therapist and patient directed toward meaning.

Paradoxical Intention

Frankl began to develop and practice paradoxical intention in the thirties. His first publication about paradoxical intention appeared in the *Schweizer Archiv für Neurologie und Psychiatrie* in 1939. He applied it primarily to phobic and obsessive-compulsive patients. It can also be tried with persons who want to change unwanted behavior patterns: stuttering, blushing, sweating, sleeplessness, or the fear of forgetting lines when making public appearances.

Paradoxical intention uses what Frankl calls "the uniquely human quality of self-detachment" (*DS*, p. 221 ff.), which enables us to step away from ourselves, look at ourselves from the outside, oppose, and even laugh at ourselves. Our capacity for self-detachment manifests itself not only in the "defiant power of the human spirit" but also in our sense of humor. Recent research by behavior therapists has shown that the logotherapeutic technique of paradoxical intention thus is mustering and mobilizing an important "coping mechanism."

In paradoxical intention, to use Frankl's definition, "patients are encouraged to do, or wish to happen, the very things they fear, even if only for a fraction of a second." The objective is to break the vicious circle that has developed as a result of anticipatory anxiety. "As soon as the fear is replaced by a paradoxical wish, the wind is taken out of the sails of anticipatory anxiety." An example from Frankl's files: A man tended to perspire easily. One day when shaking hands with his boss, he felt embarrassed that his palm was wet. About to shake someone else's hand, he was afraid it would happen again and the thought made him break out in a cold sweat. "The symptom aroused anticipatory anxiety," Frankl comments, "which intensified the symptom which, in turn, increased the fear." The vicious circle locked in its victim, the neurosis had started. "Just as the wish is the proverbial father to the thought," Frankl says, "so the fear is the mother of the neurosis."

To prepare patients for paradoxical intention, the logotherapist instructs them how the method works. If possible, they are brought together with others who were cured of the same disorder. Sentences are formulated that humorously exaggerate the consequences of the fear. The man who was afraid of perspiring, for instance, was instructed to show others his unbelievable capacity for sweating. The therapist begins with a simple demand: "Go on, show me how much you can sweat!" Then the patient takes over the formulation. "Last time I sweated only one liter," he tells himself. "This time I can easily do ten. I'll fill a bucket. Puddles will form on the floor." Eventually the patient learns to apply paradoxical intention in daily life whenever it is needed: "Tomorrow I am going to ask my boss for a raise. He will be amazed how much I can sweat."

Patients learn to apply paradoxical intention *before* they

are caught in the feared situation, at a time when they still can concentrate on formulating their phrases. They learn to phrase their formulations as true intentions ("I'll show my boss how much I can sweat!"), not as anticipation ("I'm going to sweat") because anticipation only deepens the fear.

In working out the wordings and the application of paradoxical intention, patients are supported by the therapist, but the cure comes from the patients' efforts and from the feedback that results from the disappearance of fear. They have proved to themselves that they can break the circle.

The classical application of paradoxical intention is for phobic patients. As Frankl has pointed out, phobics fear the fear; more specifically, they fear the consequences of fear—heart attacks, strokes, or a collapse. Therefore they tend to avoid fear-evoking situations. Or, in Frankl's phrase, fear of fear induces flight from fear. This pattern, then, is counteracted by paradoxical intention. To illustrate this: a man who had been afraid of open places for years was told to stop running away from the feared situation and to face it. He was instructed (after proper preparation), "You go out on the street and have yourself a juicy heart attack. It's early in the morning, you have time for two or three, and throw in a little stroke for good measure." He smiled, and the first victory was won. As Gordon Allport said, "The neurotic who learns to laugh at himself may be on the way to self-management, perhaps to cure."[4]

It makes no difference why patients decide to take a chance with paradoxical intention. They may feel they have nothing to lose; they have tried everything else. Or they may implore the therapist not to send them out to try because they see terrible consequences. The therapist then can say, "I take the responsibility that nothing will happen to you. You take the responsibility to try." In either case the patient comes back, relieved. The vicious circle is broken.

Paradoxical intention is also applied to obsessive-compulsive patients. They may be inclined to brooding, self-doubt, or scruples or may have shown a tendency to count windows, check locked doors, or repeatedly wash their hands. One day, for whatever reason, they begin to be afraid of their compulsive thoughts. They fear their behavior is the beginning of a mental disease. Or they cannot shed the thought that they may kill themselves or someone else. From then on they begin to fight their thoughts. (Frankl discusses the applications of paradoxical intention for obsessive-compulsive patients in many of his books [*MS*, p. 193 ff.; *DS*, p. 121 ff.; *WM*, p. 99 ff.; *PE*, p. 143 ff.; *UC*, p. 110 ff.; and *UC*, p. 114 ff.].) Unlike the phobic who is afraid of his fear, the obsessive-compulsive is afraid of himself. The phobic runs away from his fears, the compulsive-obsessive runs amuck against his obsessions. But pressure creates counterpressure, and the counterpressure intensifies pressure. Again a vicious circle is formed that needs to be broken. And again, exaggerated humorous formulations are worked out. For the compulsive hand washer: "All my life I have been afraid of bacteria. Now I'll make friends with them. Here I wipe my hands on the floor; I bet I can get a million of these cute little creatures on the tip of my forefinger." For the door checker: "Maybe the door is unlocked. Let the burglars come in; they need my TV more than I do. Besides, I know the door is locked anyway. I'm just an obsessive-compulsive."

Paradoxical intention, however, is applied only after a careful diagnosis. The phobic patient can be sent out on the street to "have himself a heart attack," but not if he or she is diagnosed as having a real heart condition. The *obsessive* man who only fears he will kill himself—without really intending to take his life—can tell himself to "run a dozen knives into myself until I look like a porcupine," but not a *depressive* person with actual suicidal tendencies.

The patients soon learn to handle their fears or compulsions with formulations they themselves phrase to fit the situations. They are considered cured only when they no longer need to apply paradoxical intention because the fear or compulsion has vanished. "It has happened," Lukas reports, "that patients were not able to learn paradoxical intention. It has not happened that they have mastered the techniques, and fears and compulsions still occur."[5]

Paradoxical intention is practiced at clinics in Europe, North and South America, Africa, Japan, and Australia. Hans O. Gerz, clinical director of the Connecticut Valley Hospital, reported on a six-year study of fifty-one patients, of whom almost 90 percent recovered or improved considerably after application of paradoxical intention. Recovery was rapid. Patients who had been sick for years were usually cured within one year; acute cases responded within four to twelve sessions.[6]

Recently, several therapists, including behaviorists, tested paradoxical intention against other procedures and against no treatment and a placebo. L. Michael Ascher, associate professor of psychiatry at Temple University, Philadelphia, reviewed the preliminary controlled research in the first issue of the *International Forum for Logotherapy* and concluded that paradoxical intention is a "clinically effective procedure."

The briefness of the therapy and its attention to symptoms rather than causes has aroused doubt in some psychiatric circles—unfounded, as forty years of experience show. Today most psychiatrists have come to recognize that long treatments do not necessarily produce lasting results, and the expectation that eliminated symptoms will turn up elsewhere proved unfounded. Many psychiatrists' attention to causes rather than symptoms promoted the late William Menninger to observe that it was not absolutely necessary to know the cause of a fire in order to extinguish it.

Dereflection

The third method Frankl developed is dereflection. It is applicable in cases where the symptom results from "hyperreflection" or "hyperintention," where the problem is caused by excessive attention given to a normal bodily function. A typical application is to sexual dysfunction, for which Frankl originally developed dereflection. Here again a pattern developed and has to be broken, and again it makes little difference how it started. A man may first have experienced impotence because he was tired, drunk, or whatever. It can happen to anyone. But if the next time he anxiously watches himself to see if he will have an erection, another failure is likely. If this circle is to be broken, dereflection has to be applied.

The difficulty with applying dereflection is in how to distract the patients' thoughts from their concern. How do you get an impotent man, about to have intercourse, to think about something other than his potency? How is a frigid woman in the same situation to stop observing herself in anxious anticipation of orgasm?

Frankl published an early case in 1962: Ms. S. came to him seeking help in overcoming her frigidity. As a child she had been sexually abused by her father. But it turned out not to be the traumatic childhood experience *per se* that had caused her frigidity. Influenced by popular psychoanalytical articles, she had expected the trauma to cause sexual neurosis. Frankl told her he would accept her as a patient but could not start the treatment for two months. In the meantime he told her not to worry about her dysfunction— it would be cured in the course of her treatment. But he advised her to see to it that her husband was not shortchanged, to pay attention to *his* sexual pleasure. As Frankl had foreseen, Ms. S. came back two days later, reporting she had experienced orgasm for the first time. Shifting attention from herself to her partner had resulted in the very thing she had prevented by her hyperintention and hyperreflection.

In one of my ten-week seminars I had occasion to improvise the application of dereflection. After my third lecture a young woman approached me: Her male friend had trouble with his potency, and they were to go on a weekend together. Could she try dereflection? I advised her to use a "trick" Frankl has used with his patients. She should tell her friend she was on medication, and the doctor had instructed her not to have sexual intercourse for three weeks. They were allowed any erotic activity except coitus. I also told her to let nature take its course if she saw her partner was ready. The next week she reported success. Dereflecting her friend from his performance had taken the pressure off him. There had been a moment of crisis when she had given him the go-ahead and he was worried about her doctor's orders. She told him to go ahead; she would explain later. Before the seminar ended, however, she reported a relapse, which she had handled. Since he knew about the trick with the doctor's fake orders, she had told him she had trouble with *her* orgasm and asked him to help her with it. Again dereflection had worked by shifting his attention from himself to his partner. What pleased me about this "case" was the proof that once a person understands the principles behind logotherapy one can adjust the application without further help from the therapist.

Frankl found some forty years ago what recent research has confirmed: that what lies at the root of sexual dysfunction is anticipatory anxiety of sexual failure, excessive intention of sexual performance, and excessive attention to sexual experience. Accordingly, he recommended avoiding situations that place an impotent patient in a setting where he or she feels under pressure to perform. The pressure can come from the partner (sexual demands), the situation (a weekend together), or the patient (a sexual "schedule"). Such pressure must be avoided and the patient tactfully led away from self-reflection and sex intention until the spontaneity of the sex act is restored.

Both dereflection and paradoxical intention break unwanted patterns. Paradoxical intention makes use of the human capacity for self-detachment (looking at ourselves from the outside, with a sense of humor); dereflection makes use of the human capacity for self-transcendence (reaching beyond ourselves to other human beings or to meanings). As Frankl puts it, paradoxical intention enables patients to laugh their neuroses away while dereflection enables them to look past their symptoms.

Psychological Hypochondriacs

Dereflection—shifting from oneself—is in one sense the opposite approach to that of orthodox psychoanalysis, which asks patients to concentrate on themselves. Freud faced a different situation from that facing psychiatrists today. Freud had to convince the public and the medical profession that sicknesses can be caused via the psyche in *biologically* healthy people. Frankl now has to convince the public and the medical profession that sicknesses can be caused via the *noös* in *psychologically and biologically* healthy people. But so successful was Freud in convincing his contemporaries that a neurosis is rooted in the psyche that many people suspect a psychological disorder when they are noölogically frustrated or existentially empty and anxious. In addition, some people consider others with whom they do not get along or with whom they disagree to be sick.

Freud himself laid the groundwork for the widespread feeling that "everyone is a little crazy." "Every normal person," he wrote in *Collected Papers*, "is only approximately normal; his ego resembles that of the psychotic in one point or another." Or, in *An Outline of Psychoanalysis*: "There is scarcely any condition generally recognized as normal in which it would not be possible to demonstrate neurotic traits." Erich Fromm, in *Escape from Freedom*, states that "the phenomena which we observe in the neurotic person are in principle not different from those we find in the normal." Popular conception, fed by the mass media, magnified and falsified these statements to mean we had better watch ourselves or some hidden evil will overwhelm us. Frankl takes the example of the movie, *The Snake Pit,* to point out how the movie could start anxiety feelings in a perfectly healthy woman who, after seeing the film, may start wondering: "Didn't my mother, too, when she nursed me, let me wait, or did not my father also break my doll—did I not suffer hurts similar to those of the heroine in the movie? Of course, I do not remember—but the woman in the film did not consciously know either about these childhood incidents until analysis brought them out." And so starts the vicious circle that leads from anxiety to a phobic fear of insanity. Overattention to mental health, just as overattention to happiness or sleep, will result in the opposite of what was intended: Worry about health will result in hypochondriasis, which is a sickness.

As a consequence of such misapplied logic, we now live in a society of psychological hypochondriacs, in which people go through life with their ears cocked to what is going on in their own unconscious and in the unconscious of the people around them, looking for the "true" motivations of their actions, feelings, and thoughts. Readers of *Man's Search for Meaning* often express relief at the assurance that suffering, including childhood suffering, does not necessarily lead to "complexes" and neuroses. A student in Alabama wrote Frankl about her unhappy childhood. Her parents were divorced and she had been passed on to boarding schools and summer camps. Then she commented, "I have suffered more from the thought that I should have complexes rather than from actually having them. I wouldn't trade my experiences for anything and I believe a lot of good came from them."

Many people succumb to the complexes they feel they "should have," considering their childhood experiences, and observe others for the neuroses they "ought to have." A marriage counselor said that the advice he gives most often to couples seeking help is, "Don't analyze each other!" People are sent to psychiatrists and counselors for reasons that have little to do with mental health—children who are underperforming in school, workers who are "troublemakers," and women who have illegitimate children. Leonard J. Duhl, director of the Professional Service Branch of the National Institute of Mental Health, declared that he was "tired of seeing so many issues being put on the shoulders of us psychiatrists. . . . They have, for example, accepted 'delinquency' as a mental health problem," which, he added, was really a social problem that should be dealt with through urban renewal, job opportunities, education, and other fields that have nothing to do with psychology.[7] One of the most outspoken critics of the everyone-runs-to-the-psychiatrist view is Thomas S. Szasz, professor of psychiatry at the State University of New York's Upstate Medical Center, who said that many patients come to psychiatrists with "mental diseases" that are really nothing but problems of living. In such cases, Szasz said, the physician has nothing to diagnose but rather must judge whether the person is sick or simply different, confused, difficult, or unhappy.[8]

Some psychiatrists are so indoctrinated with orthodox Freudian views that they see sickness behind any unusual behavior. A six-year-old girl suddenly refused to speak in class. The school psychologist, investigating her speaking, eating, and other "oral habits," recommended analysis. The father refused because the child seemed normal in every other way. She was transferred to a different class, where she spoke without trouble. It turned out she had been shy and the teacher and some children in her original class had made fun of her, so she had withdrawn. The school psy-

chologist foresaw that the "deep-seated problem," if not resolved in analysis, would emerge in other symptoms. Today
the young lady is married, a mother, and a perfectly well
adjusted person.

The Limits of Demasking

The purpose of the Socratic dialogue is to help patients
discover their true and evolving self under the masks they
have put on for self-protection. Freud and his disciples have
done much to lift those masks and let us look at ourselves,
including our drives and instincts. They pointed at the hidden, unadmitted, and often not very noble reasons that
make us act the way we do; and they focused on the shock-
ing impulses that motivate our thoughts and deeds. It was
healthy to release the repressed and unmask the concealed,
and Gordon W. Allport gives credit to Freud for being "a
specialist in precisely those motives that must not be taken
at their face value."[9] Now, sixty years later, however,
throwing out false motives no longer is the principal problem. The problem is to keep us from throwing out, together
with the falseness, the treasures of truth that Freud set out
to find. Freud himself occasionally went pretty far in his debunking. In his *Collected Papers* he defines parental love as
"nothing but parental narcissism born again" and friendship as "a sublimation of homosexual attitudes." But he also
knew that the search for underlying motives can be over-
done. The story is told that once at the beginning of a lecture he held up a cigar and admonished his audience: "Remember, a cigar may also be sometimes a cigar, and nothing
but a cigar."[10]

Frankl and his contemporaries are no longer concerned
with throwing out Victorian face-saving masks but with the
true face behind those masks. As Frankl put it in *Man's
Search for Meaning:* "Unmasking and debunking should stop

as soon as one is confronted with what is authentic and genuine in man, such as his desire for a life that is as meaningful as possible. If it does not stop then, the man who does the debunking merely betrays his own will to depreciate the spiritual aspirations of another" (*MS*, p. 156).

10. The Reality of Religion

Two things draw me to reverence: the starry heaven above and the moral law within.

IMMANUEL KANT

In psychotherapy the first step is to face reality. Logotherapy, an existential form of psychotherapy, maintains that reality encountered in its fullness includes the suprahuman dimension in which ultimate meaning is located. This may sound radical for orthodox psychiatry. Freud's position on religion was expressed in a letter to his friend, Ludwig Binswanger: "I have found a place for religion, by putting it under the category of the neurosis of mankind."[1] Carl Jung, however, considered religiosity not a symptom of a neurosis but a possible way to a cure. Abraham Maslow states, "Contemporary existential and humanistic psychologists would probably consider a person sick or abnormal in an existential way if he were *not* concerned with these religious questions."[2] Thus psychologists since Freud have reversed themselves. Freud considered persons sick if they were religious; Maslow considers them sick if they are unconcerned with religious questions; Frankl sees religion as expression of "man's will to meaning"—a manifestation of a "will to ultimate meaning." Albert Einstein said, "What is the meaning of human life? To find a satisfactory answer to this question is to be religious."[3] Preston Harold, in *The Shining Stranger*, states, "In the development of logotherapy, Viktor Frankl has opened the psychiatrist's door not only to any one particular religion, but to religion itself. In his work one can see the dawn of a new day in psychology's history. Recognizing Freud's contributions but moving beyond them, he has transcended psychology's old 'theology' and its 'existential vacuum.'"[4]

The Suprahuman Dimension

We have always known—at least as long as there are records of human thought—about the existence of a dimension inaccessible to the human mind. Such knowledge is personal and firsthand. Although momentary glimpses may come to anyone, deeper insights into the suprahuman dimension have been attained by prophets, mystics, and artists. All important religions are based on their founders' direct, personal visions. They then passed on their insights to their disciples. In order to be transmitted, the original visions of the prophets were enshrined in commandments and dogma. Even this indirect contact with the suprahuman helped believers in their search for meaning.

Frankl speaks of a "search for ultimate meaning" and offers a system and a terminology that allow us to discuss a subject many people today refuse to discuss in traditional terms. In addition to the three dimensions of human existence—the biological, psychological, and noölogical (or specifically human)—logotherapy speaks of the suprahuman dimension, which we cannot enter but whose edge we can touch. In this suprahuman dimension dwells the order which I have defined as ultimate meaning. One could also call is "suprameaning"—an order whose laws we can violate only at our peril, regardless of whether we see the order in religious or secular terms: as God, Life, Nature, or the Ecosystem.

Actually, "touching the edge" is misleading because it gives the impression there exists a gap between the human and suprahuman dimension. Frankl sees the "higher" dimension not as higher in any hierarchical or moralistic sense but as the more inclusive dimension. He compares the human dimension with a square that is part of a cube. The cube includes the square but goes an entire dimension beyond it. In the same way the suprahuman dimension contains the human yet transcends it. Just as an animal cannot understand the human world from its animal dimension, we cannot understand the suprahuman and its motivations. Frankl uses the following simile: "If I point to something with my finger, the dog does not look in the direction in which I point, it looks at my finger and sometimes snaps at [it.] And what about man? Is not he, too, unable to understand the meaning of something, say, the meaning of suffering, and does not he, too, quarrel with his fate and snap at its finger" (*WM*, p. 145)?

This concept of human nature may provide an intellectual understanding of the relationship between the human and the divine, but we need more. We need the actual experience of transcendence. This experience, reported by mystics since biblical times, is the subject of psychological research. Abraham Maslow, who has pioneered this research, found that such peak experiences of awareness of a higher dimension are not limited to an elect group. After interviewing many persons, he concluded that everyone can and does have such transcendent experiences, although for some they are less intense than for others, and that some people repress them, considering them a sign of insanity or at least instability. Others disregard them because such experiences do not fit their preconceived, logically built-up world view and because such people may be ultraconservative, materialistic, mechanistic, rational, or antiemotional.

Peak experiences in one ecstatic moment illuminate the mystery of existence and give us a feeling of participation in the whole, a glimpse of assurance, a fleeting awareness of a plan of which we are a part, a meaning. One peak experience can give us the courage to "say yes to life in spite of everything," to quote the title of another of Frankl's untranslated books. It can help us perceive potentials, opportunities, and tasks awaiting us. It can brighten drabness and give content to emptiness, reveal the beauty in a pine needle, uncover the significance of a word, bring about a true encounter with a stranger (or with someone who had been a stranger), and illuminate the true meaning of a situation. Such an experience can fuse two totally unconnected events and thoughts into a whole that makes us momentarily aware of unknown connections everywhere and helps us see ourselves as a vital piece in the complex jigsaw puzzle of the universe. We have to look for our own place in this puzzle, knowing there are many places into which we almost fit but only one in which we really belong.

Every living creature has this desire to be itself and have its place in the universe, but only humans are conscious of this desire. The consciousness of our religious search gives us feelings of guilt, anxiety, frustration, and emptiness but also of meaning, fulfillment, and happiness. Maslow found that these meaning-creating and blissful experiences may occur anywhere, any time, and are not limited to "holy" places and "sacred" circumstances. They produce emotional satisfaction and may even cure mental illness. He tells of two patients, one suffering from a chronic anxiety neurosis and the other from a strong obsession with suicide, who were immediately and permanently cured by one peak experience. The patients *saw* meaning, experienced it firsthand, not by thinking about it or accepting someone else's experience. A peak experience is direct and personal; it is like discovering for the first time that the color "red" exists and is wonderful. "Joy exists," Maslow comments, "can be experienced and feels very good indeed, and one can always hope that it will be experienced again."[5]

Reality and Mental Health

Personal awareness of the suprahuman dimension can give us assurance that order exists (even if it is not always manifest on the human level) and that we personally have a place in that order. The question "What is reality and what is my role?" confronts the atheist as well as the religious fundamentalist. Although their answers differ, they will be based on the same assumption, namely, that there is order, participation, and relationship in the universe. Our world must hang together or neurosis will result. A deep, personal conviction, even if it remains unconscious, pervades the orthodox believer, the liberal religionist, and the nonreligious scientist. A woman in a seminar expressed it very simply: "If faith in God gives me strength, then my God exists; he is real and near." A man sitting next to her, who had identified himself as an atheist, agreed, "Yes, but one does not need to believe in an anthropomorphic God to have that kind of faith. One can see order in the world in humanistic terms, or in terms of ultimate meaning." Science, too, rests on the assumption that the universe hangs together. Without this faith no scientist could experiment.

Reality does not depend on our faith, approval, or understanding. It is often glimpsed by lone individuals who disagree with majority belief. No measure of consensus makes reality true. Everyone saw witches at Salem, but only one St. Paul and one Einstein had glimpses of truth. Seeing is not always believing, nor is it always a good foundation of belief. Our senses tell us that the earth stands still and railroad tracks meet in the distance. None of our senses tells us that the tides are caused by the moon or that matter consists mostly of empty space. Nothing in our everyday experience gives us reason to suspect that water is made of hydrogen and oxygen. Granite seems solid but it may not be any more solid than the disc created by the fast-rotating blades of an electric fan. Motion can appear as solid matter.

Science can investigate and understand the reality of the human dimension. The reality of the suprahuman lies beyond scientific research; yet it too exists, regardless of our understanding or even our ability to understand. This existential interpretation of the suprahuman goes back to biblical times, when the writer of Exodus 3:14 has God say to Moses, "I am that I am." Regardless of what mortals feel or speculate, reality is what it is. Reality in the human dimension has not changed from the Stone Age to the space age; only our understanding has changed. America existed before Columbus, and the earth rotated around the sun before Copernicus. Suprahuman reality, too, exists, regardless of how many people believe in it and what form their belief takes. But while our ideas about reality have no effect on reality, our growing understanding of it affects our mental health. A medieval man, believing that the earth was flat and that he literally would burn eternally for his sins, was mentally healthy. He would not be considered healthy today. We define as sane a person whose ideas of reality are not too far out of step with current knowledge. Considering the recent vast and rapid changes in our understanding of the physical world and religious concepts, it is not surprising that our sanity is under more than normal strain. Refusal to see reality beyond the merely human dimension can result in feelings of emptiness, meaninglessness, frustration, loneliness, and guilt. To counter these dangers, logotherapy by no means "prescribes" religion; it simply draws attention to the fact that religion—in whatever form—cannot be excluded from the many ways in which humans have found and still can find meaning.

When the first popular article on logotherapy was published in the United States in 1954, Karl A. Menninger, educational director of the Menninger Foundation, commented, "Perhaps it is true that we psychiatrists are so afraid of endorsing religiosity and encouraging hypocrisy that we sometimes unwittingly contribute to the shyness of our patients in respect to such thoughts and communications."[6] Frankl has confirmed this shyness. He repeatedly found that patients who did not hesitate to discuss their sex life before a class of students became withdrawn when it came to discussing their religious beliefs. Repressed sex, thanks to Freud, has been released from many of its shackles; but repressed religiosity is on the increase.

Frankl, no more interested in making his patients religionists than Freud was in making them sexualists, wants neither to promote nor to discourage religious views in a patient. He has compared the search for meaning to a train ride. Logotherapy does not provide final stations in the form of ultimate answers; it leads patients, the religious as well as the nonreligious, to a point where they can find their own transfers to stations beyond, to their own ultimate station. The terminal of logotherapy—meaning—lies in the direction of true religiosity. "To genuine religiousness man cannot be driven by an instinct," Frankl states, "nor pushed by a psychiatrist" (*UG*, p. 72). For the therapist to give answers is not only inappropriate, it is unnecessary. Logotherapy has demonstrated repeatedly that the effect of answers about life's meaning are incomparably deeper if they come from the patient, not from the therapist.

Logotherapists must not restrict the patient's choice. They must remain entirely neutral on the patient's religious decisions. "Logotherapy," says Frankl, "simply states: man is searching. But it can never decide if he is searching for a God he has invented, for a God he has discovered, for a God he cannot find, or for himself."[7]

Beyond the Reach of Science

Science, which was expected to disprove the existence of a suprahuman dimension, has on the contrary brought into focus the limits of human reach and therefore pointed up the existence of a dimension that lies beyond. Today scientists' logic has joined the prophets' vision in indicating the existence of a reality beyond human grasp. Scientific discovery can go only as far as the limits of the human dimension. To reach the reality that lies beyond requires a leap. Even a scientifically oriented work such as the *Encyclopedia Americana* states, "How matter itself came into being is not a scientific question—its presence has to be assumed." When scientists reach the limits of the human dimension, they are faced with alternatives, none of which can be resolved on the human level. The reality of the universe is an undisputable fact, but it is based on a mystery unsolvable in the human dimension. The astronomer George Gamov points out that either there was a moment in time when something was created from nothing or this creative moment never happened because "something" (even if only in the form of energy) always existed. Thus the choice is between alternatives, both beyond human experience: nothingness and timelessness.

The concept of time points up the difference between the human and the suprahuman dimension. On the human level time is easily understood: everything has a beginning and an end; our temporality begins at birth and ends with death; history is a string of events taking place in time; we can even understand the mystery of the now moving forever on the crest of the wave between the past, which no longer exists, and the future, which does not yet exist. But we cannot comprehend eternal time, although we know it exists. We know that time goes back before our birth, before the existence of life on earth, before the existence of the earth itself. We know it will go on after our death, after the end of life on earth, and after the end of the earth. We know that eternity exists, but it is unimaginable and incomprehensible. Frankl speaks of it as "supratime." Eternity is not a time *after* our limited time; it lies in a different dimension. Time, according to Frankl's concept, is to eternity as the hand of a clock is to its dial—a one-dimensional line to a two-dimensional plane.

The same can be said about space. We can understand human space but not infinity, which is not merely space beginning where finite space ends. It lies in another dimension, above finite space, although finite space is as much part of the infinite as the square is part of the cube. Eternity and infinity are incomprehensible on the human level; yet they are more than theoretical concepts. Our personal experience with our own human temporality and spatial limitations gives us some participation in the higher dimension where eternity and infinity exist. In a similar manner we can participate in perfect beauty by looking for and experiencing beautiful things on the human level, partake of absolute truth through the millions of truths we find, and take part in ultimate meaning through searching for the meanings of individual life situations. To reach meaning, truth, or infinity is beyond us. We can approach the suprahuman one step at a time, but we remain limited in our human dimension.

Although science cannot reach the suprahuman, it can extend the human dimension and have an impact on religious belief. The great discoveries of the fifteenth century, the opening up of the globe, revolutionized our ideas of life on earth and brought about the Reformation, which reshaped our religious concepts. The beginning space discoveries and the opening up of the universe (even on the minute scale accessible to us) could bring a religious reformation on a vaster scale. Space science indicates the immense gap between human and suprahuman laws by showing that the physical laws we experience on earth do not apply even a short distance beyond it. Gravity no longer holds true for the astronaut after only a brief hop into space. Gravity, the most universal earthly law, is a rare exception; it exists only near stars and planets. If we are ever able to journey to the stars, we will travel for years without getting close enough to those rare clumps of matter around which gravity exists. Children born in such a spaceship may well believe that the reality of gravity does not exist because it is beyond their experience. We are entering a reality in which up merges with down, where we must orient by points of reference in continuous motion, where we wear magnetic shoes in order to stay on the "ground." For the first time we are experiencing a world of constant motion, constant change, a world of relativity in the presence of majestic order. We may be living in the pristine moments of a spiritual space age, wherein we will need noëtic shoes of gravity to orient ourselves in a world without spiritual gravity. We will need a new orientation, without the familiar points of reference and without the traditional laws of nature. In such a world the survival of the fittest may no longer mean the biologically strongest or the instinctually surest, but strongest in their humanness. Only those who can find the meanings of the radically changed situation may survive, just as the mammals survived in the times of the changed physical conditions of the ice age.

If gravity is not universal, if a baby born in a spaceship can grow up with no experience of this—for earthlings—inescapable physical law, what can we say about moral laws, about ultimate meaning and purpose? Perhaps we earthlings are travelers in space for whom moral laws are beyond experience. Yet in a different dimension moral laws and ultimate meaning exist.

The Vanishing Point

That ultimate meaning (*logos*) resides in the divine dimension, perhaps even *is* the divine dimension, is no invention of logotherapy. It is as old as the Gospel. John 1:1 states, "In the beginning was logos. Logos was with God and logos was divine." Logos traditionally is translated as "the word." Frankl translates it as "meaning." In his translation the biblical passage reads, "In the beginning was ultimate meaning, and meaning was with God, and meaning was divine." To our biblical ancestors the core of the universe was the word of God, which under the priests' influence became a static concept. In our retranslation the core of the universe is meaning, a dynamic concept; and we can only hope it will not become fossilized in dogma, too. Contemporary Bible scholars no longer translate the previously quoted definition of God as "I am that I am" but as "I shall be that I shall be," indicating continuous evolution even on the highest level of existence. In this era of relativity, it is conceivable that even the divine force (regarded in the past as the essence of the absolute) may be evolving and continuously expanding, as does the physical universe. In this era of free search for reality, God is seen as ground of our existence as well as its goal—not a static and absolute goal but one expanding, coaxing, guiding, and challenging.

Frankl describes God's existence as analogous to the vanishing point in a drawing: "All lines in the picture converge on it; it dominates the picture but is not really 'in' it."[8] Applying this analogy to our existence, we might say that in wandering through life we move toward the vanishing point but never reach it. It coaxes us along and expands with the horizon. We can reach landmarks in the physical landscape but never the vanishing point itself.

Frankl also uses the concept of the vanishing point to explain the relationship between meanings on the human level and ultimate meaning on the suprahuman level, that unreachable yet always beckoning goal. He suggests that if we consistently follow those "meaning lines" of our human existence, one point ought to emerge toward which they run. Although we never can reach that point, we strive toward it. This may be the way, he speculates, in which the most important Hebrew prayer ("Our Lord is One") is to be understood in its deepest sense: "To perceive all meaning as converging into a highest Meaning which, for lack of another term, we call God, so that every truth, thought to the end, means God, and all beauty, loved to the end, sees God."[9]

A Personal God

God as vanishing point, as the eternal present, as an impersonal evolving force, to many people is an interesting intellectual exercise without relevance to their personal lives. It has been said that existential philosophy and psychology secularize religion. But they also religionize the secular. They broaden the spectrum of personal experiences from which we find meaning and thus broaden the base of religion so that it becomes acceptable to more people.

In biblical times religion was all-encompassing—nothing in human experience was outside it. People personally experienced God in every aspect of their lives, in the richness of their harvest and in famines, in the beauty of a sunset and the terror of a thunderstorm, in dreams and visions, in the ravages by an enemy and the love of a father. God himself was seen as a father, strict and loving, rewarding and punishing according to laws beyond human understanding. People were children of God, secure in their knowledge that they were important enough for God to watch over them personally and to judge every action. This feeling of being cared about and being part of a whole was the basis for mental health.

Religious traditions preserved this God concept, and for millions it continues to provide security. Others, however, doubt their childhood belief in the father and, like adolescents, revolt against the father image of divine reality. But as psychology points out, rejection of the father image, even his death, does not free the child from its reality. Children achieve freedom from their father not by running away but by understanding him. The truth that makes us free evolves slowly—by religious insight, scientific investigation, and personal search.

Existential philosophy and psychology expand our freedom of choice. The evolving truth is also freeing us from concepts of the divine that are no longer relevant. It makes us free to check new religious hypotheses against personal experience.

Individual freedom and personal responsibleness are playing an increasing part in our search for ultimate meaning. To believers in a father God, it is he who demands and enforces responsibility. Nonbelievers, however, point to the findings of psychology that a loving as well as a tyrannical father can enslave the child and keep him or her from accepting responsibleness. We realize that God's glory is not diminished when we accept personal responsibleness, just as God does not need our supplication in order to be great. God's universal responsibleness prods us to take on that share within our own finite realm. The religious person says, "God helps those who help themselves." An atheist expressed it in his way: "Religion's function is to prompt us to be good. Personal responsibility can take this function. If no one watches, everything is permitted. If God doesn't watch, our own conscience can. Personal responsibility can replace a personal God."

Thus the atheist calls for a theology that replaces a personal God with personal responsibleness. The atheist says to be ethical we have to respond to our conscience; the religious person says to be saved we have to respond to God. The logotherapist maintains that to be healthy we have to respond. Whether we conceive the demand to which we respond as coming from a personal God or a personal responsibleness is for each person to decide.

Our Relationship to the Divine

Depth psychology has shown we can lose our relationship with the unknown in our psyche; and "height" psychology, such as logotherapy, is showing that we may also lose our relationship with meanings and values. Life becomes meaningless when we deny or repress our relationship with ultimate meaning.

This is the paradox of the religious search; we know a divine dimension exists, can never find out what it is, and yet are thirsting to find a relationship with this mystery. The religious base, whether we call it God, universal order, or ultimate meaning, cannot crumble, give way, or end because it is eternal and limitless. It is not under us like a safety net or above us like a protective roof, but we are part of it like a temporal cell in an eternal body. The cell cannot isolate itself on the ground that it never saw the heart that supplies it with blood. Our relationship with the divine is inescapable, but it is up to us to become aware of it on a personal level of understanding. Even the atheist cannot abolish this relationship. Atheism is a denial of a personal God rather than of an ultimate meaning.

Today religion has become as existential as it was at the time of the Bible: not concerned with religious theories but with daily experience. Our concern—and modern theology stresses this—is how to live up to our potentials, how to bear unavoidable suffering, how to live in the face of inescapable uncertainty, how to find meaning and content. In times like the present theoretical religious concepts such as heaven and immortality become less relevant than the reality of the religious search.

In contrast to the scientific search for truth, the religious search is aimed at a goal beyond our understanding. And yet it is in our nature to pursue it; we would lose our humanness if we discontinued the pursuit. Religion is our relationship with the unknowable, our dialogue with transcendence. In this dialogue we need not, even cannot, understand the questions clearly; yet we must be ready to respond. In *Between Man and Man*, Buber said, "He who ceases to make a response, ceases to hear the Word."

We have learned that to demand *the* answer will bring frustration, but the continuing effort to find *an* answer may bring fulfillment. Because final answers lie in a suprahuman dimension, we must be content in finding answers to concrete questions in concrete situations. We learn to appraise our shortcomings realistically and realize that our great opportunity lies in our incompleteness, our chance to grow, change, evolve. We realize we are unique not because we are so wonderful but because each of us is free to respond uniquely. The emphasis, in short, has shifted from God's demands, which in their totality are unknowable, toward our response to what, to the best of our abilities, we conceive God's commands to be—and to respond to them one at a time in each situation. We know the limitations of our freedom—our dependence on biological, psychological, and environmental influences—and we realize that to reproach ourselves for failure to reach achievements beyond our natural limitations is not religion but masochism. To fall short is not a sin or mental sickness but a natural consequence of being human. Our shortcomings become sins only when we ignore them, do not learn from them, or refuse to change.

The Proof of the Divine

In our search for individual meaning lines, the existence of a higher dimension is always presupposed, even by atheists. What most atheists reject is not a suprahuman dimension but a traditional concept of God. A few go further and reject all nontangible reality because they cannot see it. Such a young nonbeliever approached Frankl in 1945. The young man had become disillusioned by the ravages and cruelties of war and cried out, "How can I believe in God? I cannot acknowledge that there is spirit, God, a soul. Show me a soul. I cannot see it, not even through a microscope. I see tissues of brain, but no soul." Frankl asked him what had motivated him to search for the soul. The youth said that it was his desire to find the truth. "Is this desire of yours tangible?" Frankl asked him. "Will it be visible under a microscope?" "Of course not," the young man admitted, "because it is mental. You don't see mental things under a microscope." "Ah," said Frankl, "in other words, what you were in vain searching for in the microscope, had been a precondition for your search, and presupposed all along" (*WM*, p. 151).

In Frankl's view religion is our presupposition of a suprahuman dimension and our basic trust that ultimate meaning dwells in that dimension. Yet the demand for "proof" persists. Such proof comes only through experiencing the things that escape logical arguments. Frankl has tried a phenomenological approach to prove the existence of the divine dimension, that is, a proof based on the description of actual phenomena. He starts with Pascal's, "I would not seek Thee if I had not already found Thee." We have an emotional need to seek the suprahuman dimension, a need that can be explained only by an unconscious precognition that this suprahuman dimension exists. Frankl then turns to the phenomenon of love, pointing out that love, too, must be preceded by a lovable object. This, Frankl concedes, is not a logical proof. He compares it with Descartes' proof of human existence: "I think, therefore I am." Frankl suggests that we may paraphrase Descartes: "I love [God], therefore

He is." Just as Descartes deduces the existence of the self from the act of thinking, so we may deduce God's infinite existence from our infinite love.

Such inference of the existence of God will not come easily to people who are not ready for religious experiences, who have shut the doors on them, or who have "repressed their metaphysical needs." The religious believer not only believes in the existence of God but is convinced that some belief in the suprahuman is held by everybody, even if only in the unconscious. This is not so absurd a statement as it may seem at first glance. Does not everyone, for instance, believe in the thou of another person, although this thou, the spiritual basis of body and psyche, remains invisible? The God of the believer is something like the primary thou, the invisible essence behind the manifestations. Coming home to Vienna after his experiences in the death camps, Frankl wrote, "God is the primary, the ultimate Thou to such an extent that one cannot truly speak *of* God, in the third person, but only *to* him, in the second. I cannot imagine that a man who stood in a war trench or in a death camp and spoke to God can later stand in a lecture hall and speak of God as if this were the same one he had spoken to directly, in the trench."[10]

To speak to God is an event that eliminates the necessity of proof. But such an experience is the only possible proof of a phenomenon that exists in a dimension inaccessible to reason. "From petrified footprints you may infer that dinosaurs have existed" says Frankl. "But from natural things you cannot infer that a supernatural being exists. God is no petrification" (*WM*, p. 148). God is not something that exists as other things exist in the human dimension. He exists in a different dimension altogether; He is the ground of existence. It may be, speculates Frankl, that God "is" not in any dimension at all—He may be the coordinate system itself.

To attempt to prove the existence of God as we would the

existence of prehistoric animals would mean to reduce the divine to the human or physical level. The absurdity of such reductionism is illustrated in a story of a little boy who told Frankl that he had decided what he was going to be when he grew up. "I shall be," he said, "either a trapeze artist or God." The boy, says Frankl, had disregarded the dimensional difference; he dealt with God as if being God were one vocation among others.

One need not be a child to fall into the trap of reducing God to the human dimension. On a more sophisticated level this is also done by those who expect God to answer their prayers or by those who declare that God is dead. To expect a direct answer from God, Frankl declares, is magical thinking. "If you have a ship and wish to probe how deep the ocean is, you send down a wave of sound, and it is reflected. And when you get the echo, you know it comes from the bottom of the ocean. However, God is infinite depth."[11] That is why you should not be astonished that God is silent. "God is not dead—He is silent" (*WM*, p. 154).

The "Language" of Religion

Religion is at one and the same time universal and personal, like language. Human language is a universal phenomenon, but every one of us has a personal mode of speech in a specific language. A baby babbles in universal sounds before they are narrowed to those of his or her mother tongue. The feeling of universal religion is also narrowed as a person grows up in one religious tradition.

The parallel between religion and language has fascinated Frankl through the years. In a lecture at Brandeis Institute in California, he phrased it in these words:

> You can arrive at truth through every language, but you may also err and lie in every language. It's up to you rather than to the language. The same holds for the various religions and de-

nominations. This does not do away with the strength of your convictions. It does make for humility and tolerance. You need not share the belief of someone else, but you should recognize the other person's right to have a belief of his own and to let himself be led by his own conscience and nothing else. The firmer you stand in your own creed, the more your hands will be free to reach out for others. The weaker you stand in your creed, the more you will use both hands to cling to the dogma, and you then have no hands to reach out for others.[12]

Frankl argues that we approach truth only by thinking, and we think best in our own language. Other languages may better express shades of meanings and have more words, but generally one's own language will be the best vehicle to approach the reality that lies behind all languages. Similarly, it is a mistake to believe that true religiosity can best be achieved by staying outside all denominations. A person believing this is like someone without a language. It is equally a mistake to believe the trend is toward universal religion, an artificially contrived general religion, a sort of religious Esperanto. Artificial religiosity is no religiosity at all. The trend, Frankl feels, is not toward universal religion but toward an utterly personal religion, a religion where every one of us eventually will be able to find a language of our own to communicate with the divine. Even if religion should ever become individualized to the extent that we all speak our own religious language, we will have to use the common symbols of religion, just as different languages use the same alphabet. Frankl sees a trend to religion but away from those denominations that apparently have nothing better to do than fight each other.

Old Truths Rediscovered

Rigid believers assume all that can be said about God has been frozen in a definite form and nothing can be added.

But new information pours in from all fields of inquiry, and it is unrealistic to presume that religion can be exempted. Every generation must reexamine the view of God it inherited; and this is particularly true of the young today, entering an age when the vision of the prophet, "that the foundations of the earth do shake," is—as Tillich observes—becoming an actual physical possibility and might become historical reality. Isaiah's warning that the "earth is split in pieces" is not merely a metaphor but hard reality. It is physics. "That," Tillich points out, "is the religious meaning of the age into which we have entered."[13]

It is an age of puzzling paradoxes. The protection of old traditions is wearing thin, and new ones have not yet developed. New information is thrown at us from all sides, conflicting with cherished beliefs. We are finally reaping the full consequences of Adam's and Eve's eating from the Tree of Knowledge and their expulsion from the garden, where all paths had been marked and where they had been guided by instincts. We now live in a world of unmarked paths where at every crossroad we must make decisions. We have vastly increased our freedom, but the knowledge to find our way is still limited. We feel anxiety because the burden of freedom is great, and guilt because in every choice we know we could have chosen otherwise. We feel the pull forward, toward more freedom and knowledge, but also the longing for the security of the marked paths of the dim past. This two-way pull tears us apart, even more painfully because the guidance of tradition is failing. A return to the garden is blocked. We cannot relinquish our freedom, unlearn our knowledge, or suppress our urge to reach out if we want to remain human. We have to accept expulsion, not as punishment but as challenge. In Buber's words (*Way of Response*), "The flaming sword of the cherubim circling the entrance of Paradise prohibits the way back. But it also illuminates the way forward."

Logotherapy helps illuminate the way forward, step by step, for each person individually. It tells us we cannot change our past, but we are not its slave either. We can change our present and influence our future. We have limitations but also freedom within these. To use this freedom can make the difference between a full and an empty life; but if not used responsibly, freedom will turn into meaningless arbitrariness. We have choices at every moment and must make them in the face of constant uncertainty; we cannot wait until all the answers are in. We are alone, yet we participate in a reality that far transcends our understanding. Life does not owe us pleasure but offers us meanings. Logotherapy tells us we can never grasp the reality of the ultimate, whatever name it is given; but everything depends on how we respond to its demands. Ultimate meaning exists but is ultimately unknowable for the individual. We can approach it through our conscience, which is part of the human makeup and therefore can err. Our best efforts will reveal not the overall master plan but only the meaning of one life situation at a time. We participate in ultimate meaning only by responding, to the best of our limited capacities, to the meaning demands of the moment. The day-by-day pursuit of meaning gives content to our lives. Happiness, peace of mind, satisfaction, and success are only by-products of our pursuit of meaning.

Brief summaries of logotherapy, like the above, provoke claims that none of this is new. Frankl is aware of this reaction. He recalls, "When I first lectured in the United States, people told me that what I presented was something new, at least as compared with psychoanalysis. But later, on my tours in Asia, in India and Japan, I was told the contrary. People pointed out to me that what I was saying were old truths one might find in the ancient Vedas, in Zen, or in the writings of Laotse."[14]

He considers both these evaluations of logotherapy justified and feels complimented on both counts. "It's an honor if people regard my contributions as something new, but it is equally an honor when they see old truths in logotherapy. Karl Jaspers once remarked that in philosophy something wholly new is likely not to be fully true. That holds for psychotherapy, too. If logotherapy has achieved nothing more than to rediscover and reformulate old truths, it will have contributed to the advancement of psychotherapy. But I think logotherapy has taken a step further: it has made the old wisdom into a system and a method, and thus made it teachable and learnable. Seen in this light both evaluations of logotherapy, by Americans as well as Asians, may be correct: old truths have had to be rediscovered and reformulated in a systematic and methodologically refined way so we can apply them to our own lives."[15]

Notes

Text references to those of Viktor Frankl's books available in English use the following symbols:

MS—*Man's Search for Meaning*
DS—*The Doctor and the Soul*
WM—*The Will to Meaning*
PE—*Psychotherapy and Existentialism*
UG—*The Unconscious God*
UC—*The Unheard Cry for Meaning*

Text references to other sources are listed below.

Chapter I

1. W. S. Sahakian and B. J. Sahakian, "Logotherapy as a Personality Theory," *Israel Annals of Psychiatry* 10 (1972), pp. 230–244.
2. From author's personal communication with Frankl.
3. From Frankl's unpublished lecture notes.

Chapter II

1. From Frankl's unpublished lecture notes.
2. From author's personal recollection.
3. From case demonstration available at the Viktor E. Frankl Library and Memorabilia, Graduate Theological Union, 2465 Le Conte, Berkeley, Calif. 94709.*
4. J. C. Crumbaugh and L. T. Maholick, "An Experimental Study in Existentialism: The Psychometric Approach to Frankl's Concept of Noögenic Neurosis," *Journal of Clinical Psychology* 20 (1964), p. 200.

* English-language works of Viktor Frankl are available at the Viktor E. Frankl Library and Memorabilia, address above, attention Dr. Robert Leslie.

Chapter III

1. Viktor E. Frankl, "Logotherapie und Religion," *Christlich-Pädagogische Blätter* 79 (1966), p. 33.
2. Quoted in *DS*, page 113.
3. From author's personal communication with Frankl.
4. From author's personal communication with Frankl.
5. Edith Weisskopf-Joelson, "Logotherapy and Existential Analysis," *Acta Psychotherapeutica* 6 (1958), pp. 193–204.
6. From author's personal communication with Frankl.

Chapter IV

1. From author's personal communication with Frankl.
2. From author's personal communication with Dr. Elisabeth Lukas, logotherapist in Munich, Germany.
3. From author's personal communication with Frankl, related also, in different form, in *WM*, pp. 63–64.
4. From author's personal communication with Frankl.

Chapter V

1. Viktor E. Frankl, *Der Wille zum Sinn* (Bern-Stuttgart-Wien: Verlag Hans Huber, 1972), p. 168.
2. Gordon W. Allport, "Psychological Models for Guidance," *Harvard Educational Review* 32 (1962), p. 373.
3. From author's personal communication with Frankl.

Chapter VI

1. Abraham Maslow, *Motivation and Personality* (New York: Harper & Row, 1954), p. 60.
2. Viktor E. Frankl, *Der Wille zum Sinn*, p. 183.
3. Quoted in *WM*, page 38.
4. Charlotte Bühler, "Theoretical Observations about Life's Basic Tendencies," *American Journal of Psychotherapy* 13 (1959), p. 561.
5. Quoted editorially in "Tumult and Shouting," *San Francisco Chronicle*, April 30, 1967.
6. From Frankl's unpublished lecture notes. A similar statement is found in *WM*, page 98.

Chapter VII

1. Viktor E. Frankl, *Trotzdem Ja zum Leben Sagen.* (Wien: Franz Deuticke, 1947), p. 8.
2. Viktor E. Frankl, "Der Unternehmer im Spannungsfeld der Pathologie des Zeitgeistes," *Oesterreichische Aerztezeitung* 13 (1958), p. 922.
3. Viktor E. Frankl, "Value Dimensions in Teaching," in *Values Colloquium I, A Person's Need and Search for Values* (The Religious Education Foundation, 343 South Madison Avenue, Pasadena, CA 91106. Mimeo, February 1964).
4. Nevitt Sanford, "Psychiatry Viewed from the Outside: The Challenge of the Next Ten Years," Symposium, *American Journal of Psychiatry* 123 (1966), pp. 519–522.
5. Robert M. Hutchins, *The University in America* (Santa Barbara, Calif. Center for the Study of Democratic Institutions, 1966).
6. The remarks by Clarence Faust, Walter Lippmann, and Rosemary Parks are taken from a Conference Report published in *Center Diary* (Santa Barbara, Calif.: Center for the Study of Democratic Institutions, 1966), p. 14.

Chapter VIII

1. From author's personal recollection.
2. From unpublished remarks during the question period at San Francisco City College, San Francisco, November 5, 1978.
3. J. L. Simmons and Barry Winograd, *It's Happening* (Santa Barbara, Calif. March-Laird Publications, 1966).

Chapter IX

1. Quoted in *WM*, pp. 53–54.
2. Quoted in *WM*, p. 53.
3. Elisabeth Lukas, *An Sinnerfüllung Gesunden*, unpublished manuscript.
4. Gordon W. Allport, *The Individual and His Religion* (New York: Macmillan, 1950), p. 92.
5. Elisabeth Lukas, *Sinnerfüllung*.
6. Hans O. Gerz, "Experience with the Logotherapeutic Technique of Paradoxical Intention in the Treatment of Phobic and Obsessive-Compulsive Patients," *American Journal of Psychiatry* 123 (1966), pp. 548–553.
7. Leonard J. Duhl, *The American Character* (Santa Barbara, Calif. Center for the Study of Democratic Institutions, 1965).
8. Quoted in Edwin M. Shur, "Psychiatrists under Attack," *Atlantic* (July 1966).

9. Quoted in *WM*, p. 52.
10. Quoted in *WM*, p. 54.

Chapter X

1. Ludwig Binswanger, *Reminiscences of a Friendship* (New York: Grune & Stratton, 1957), p. 96.
2. Abraham Maslow, *Religions, Values, and Peak-Experiences* (Columbus: Ohio State University Press, 1964), p. 18.
3. Quoted in D. L. Farnsworth, "The Search for Meaning," *Academic Reporter* 5 (1960).
4. Harold Preston, *The Shining Stranger* (New York: Wayfarer Press, 1967).
5. Maslow, *Religions*, p. 56.
6. Quoted in W. Arthur Kline, "We Are Born to Believe," *Woman's Home Companion* (April, 1954).
7. Frankl, *Wille zum Sinn*, p. 75.
8. Ibid, p. 67.
9. Ibid, p. 68.
10. Ibid, p. 67.
11. Ibid, p. 69–70.
12. Viktor E. Frankl, "Three Lectures on Logotherapy." Long-playing records, Brandeis Institute, Brandeis, CA 93064.
13. Paul Tillich, *The Shaking of the Foundations* (New York: Charles Scribner's Sons, 1948), p. 3.
14. From author's personal communication with Frankl.

Bibliography

Books and Articles

Ansbacher, Rowena R. "The Third Viennese School of Psychotherapy." *Journal of Individual Psychology* 15 (1959): 236–237.

Ascher, L. Michael. "Paradoxical Intention." In *Handbook of Behavioral Interventions*, edited by A. Goldstein and E. B. Foa. New York: Wiley, in press.

Ascher, L. Michael, and Turner, Ralph M. "A Controlled Comparison of Progressive Relaxation, Stimulus Control, and Paradoxical Intention Therapies for Insomnia." *Journal of Consulting and Clinical Psychology*, in press.

Bulka, Reuven P. "Logotherapy and Talmudic Judaism." *Journal of Religion and Health* 14 (1975): 277–283.

———. "Logotherapy and the Talmud on Suffering: Clinical and Meta-Clinical Perspectives." *Journal of Psychology and Judaism* 2 (1977): 31–44.

———. "Logotherapy—A Step Beyond Freud: Its Relevance for Jewish Thought." *Jewish Life* 2 (1977–1978): 46–53.

Cohen, David. "The Frankl Meaning." *Human Behavior* (1977): 56–62.

Crumbaugh, James C. "Cross Validation of Purpose-in-Life Test Based on Frankl's Concepts." *Journal of Individual Psychology* 24 (1968): 74–81.

———. *Everything to Gain: A Guide to Self-Fulfillment Through Logoanalysis*. Chicago: Nelson-Hall, 1973.

———. "An Experimental Study in Existentialism: The Psychometric Approach to Frankl's Concept of Noögenic Neurosis." *Journal of Clinical Psychology* 20 (1964): 200–207.

———, and Russell, John. *Logotherapy: New Help For Problem Drinkers*. Chicago: Nelson-Hall, 1980.

Downing, Lester N. *Counseling Theories and Techniques*. Chicago: Nelson-Hall, 1975.

Fabry, Joseph. "Application of Logotherapy in Small Sharing Groups." *Journal of Religion and Health* 13 (1974): 128–136.

————. "The Noëtic Unconscious." *The International Forum for Logotherapy* 2 (1979), pp. 8–11.*

————. Joseph B.; Bulka, Reuven; and Sahakian, William S.; eds. *Logotherapy in Action.* New York: Jason Aronson, 1979.

Frankl, Viktor E. "Aspects and Prospects of Logotherapy." *The International Forum for Logotherapy* 1 (1978), pp. 3–6.

————. "Beyond Self-Actualization and Self-Expression." *Journal of Existential Psychiatry* 1 (1960): 5–20.

————. "The Depersonalization of Sex." In *Humanistic Psychology: A Source Book,* edited by I. David Welch, George A. Tate, and Fred Richards. Buffalo, N.Y.: Prometheus, 1978.

————. *The Doctor ånd the Soul: From Psychotherapy to Logotherapy.* New York: Knopf, 1955. Second, expanded edition, 1965. Paperback edition, New York: Vintage, 1977.

————. "Encounter: The Concept and Its Vulgarization." *The Journal of the American Academy of Psychoanalysis* 1 (1973): 73–83.

————. "Encounter: The Concept and Its Vulgarization." In *Psychotherapy and Behavior Change,* edited by Hans H. Strupp, et al. Chicago: Aldine, 1974.

————. "The Feeling of Meaninglessness: A Challenge to Psychotherapy." *The American Journal of Psychoanalysis* 32 (1972): 85–89.

————. "Logos and Existence in Psychotherapy." *American Journal of Psychotherapy* 7 (1953): 8–15.

————. "On Logotherapy and Existential Analysis." *American Journal of Psychoanalysis* 18 (1958): 28–37.

————. "Logotherapy and Existential Analysis: A Review." *American Journal of Psychotherapy* 20 (1966): 252–260.

————. *Man's Search for Meaning: An Introduction to Logotherapy.* Boston: Beacon Press, 1959. Paperback edition, New York: Pocket Books, 1977.

————. "Man's Search for Ultimate Meaning." In *On the Way to Self-Knowledge,* edited by Jacob Needleman. New York: Knopf, 1976.

* *The International Forum for Logotherapy* is published by the Institute of Logotherapy, 1 Lawson Road, Berkeley, CA 94707, and can be ordered from the Institute for $4 an issue or $18 for a subscription of six issues.

————. "Paradoxe Intention." *Schweizer Archiv für Neurologie und Psychiatrie* 43 (1939), pp. 26–31.

————. "Paradoxical Intention and Dereflection." *Psychotherapy: Theory, Research and Practice* 12 (1975): 226–237.

————. "Paradoxical Intention: A Logotherapeutic Technique." *American Journal of Psychotherapy* 14 (1960): 520–535.

————. "Paradoxical Intention: A Logotherapeutic Technique." In *Active Psychotherapy*, edited by Harold Greenwald. New York: Atherton Press, 1967.

————. "Paradoxical Intention and Dereflection: Two Logotherapeutic Techniques." In *New Dimensions in Psychiatry: A World View*, edited by Silvano Arieti. New York: Wiley, 1975.

————. "The Philosophical Foundations of Logotherapy." In *Phenomenology: Pure and Applied*, edited by Erwin Straus. Pittsburgh: Duquesne University Press, 1964.

————. *Psychotherapy and Existentialism: Selected Papers on Logotherapy*. New York: Washington Square Press, 1967. Paperback edition, New York: Touchstone, 1978.

————. "Reductionism and Nihilism." In *Beyond Reductionism: New Perspectives in the Life Sciences* (The Alpback Symposium, 1968), edited by Arthur Koestler and J. R. Smythies. New York: Macmillan, 1970.

————. "Self-Transcendence as a Human Phenomenon." *Journal of Humanistic Psychology* 6 (1966): 97–106.

————. "Self-Transcendence as a Human Phenomenon." In *Readings in Humanistic Psychology*, edited by Anthony J. Sutich and Miles A. Vich. New York: Free Press, 1969.

————. *The Unconscious God: Psychotherapy and Theology*. New York: Simon and Schuster, 1977.

————. *The Unheard Cry for Meaning: Psychotherapy and Humanism*. New York: Simon and Schuster, 1978.

————. *The Will to Meaning: Foundations and Applications of Logotherapy*. New York: World Publishing Company, 1969. Paperback edition, New York: New American Library, 1978.

Gerz, Hans O. "Experience with the Logotherapeutic Technique of Paradoxical Intention in the Treatment of Phobic and Obsessive-Compulsive Patients." *American Journal of Psychiatry* 123 (1966): 548–553.

Hall, Mary Harrington. "A Conversation with Viktor Frankl of Vienna." *Psychology Today* 1 (1968): 56–63.

Holmes, R. M. "Alcoholics Anonymous as Group Logotherapy." *Pastoral Psychology* 21 (1970): 30–36.

Hyman, William. "Practical Aspects of Logotherapy in Neurosurgery." *Existential Psychiatry* 7 (1969): 99–101.

Kimble, Melvin A. "Applications in Pastoral Psychology." *The International Forum for Logotherapy* 2 (1979), pp. 31–34.

Klitzke, Louis L. "Students in Emerging Africa: Humanistic Psychology and Logotherapy in Tanzania," *Journal of Humanistic Psychology* 9 (1969): 105–126.

Leslie, Robert C. *Jesus and Logotherapy: The Ministry of Jesus as Interpreted Through the Psychotherapy of Viktor Frankl.* New York: Abingdon, 1965.

Liston, Robert A. *Healing the Mind: Eight Views of Human Nature.* New York: Praeger, 1974.

Lukas, Elisabeth. "The 'Ideal' Logotherapist." *The International Forum for Logotherapy* 2 (1979), pp. 3–7.

––––––. "Logotherapy's Message to Parents and Teachers." *The International Forum for Logotherapy* 1 (1978), pp. 10–13.

Maslow, A. H. "Comments on Dr. Frankl's Paper." *Journal of Humanistic Psychology* 6 (1966): 107–112.

––––––. "Comments on Dr. Frankl's Paper." In *Readings in Humanistic Psychology*, edited by Anthony J. Sutich and Miles A. Vich. New York: Free Press, 1969.

Matson, Katinka. *The Psychology Omnibook of Personal Development.* New York: Morrow, 1977.

"Meaning in Life." *Time* (Feb. 2, 1968), pp. 38–40.

Meshoulam, Uriel. "Some Implications of Logotherapy on Community Health." *The International Forum of Logotherapy* 1 (1978), pp. 7–9.

Misiak, Henry, and Sexton, Virginia Staud. *Phenomenological, Existential, and Humanistic Psychologies: A Historical Survey.* New York: Grune & Stratton, 1973.

Patterson, C. H. *Theories of Counseling and Psychotherapy.* New York: Harper & Row, 1966.

Polak, Paul. "Frankl's Existential Analysis." *American Journal of Psychotherapy* 3 (1949): 517–522.

Price, Johanna. *Abnormal Psychology: Current Perspectives.* Del Mar, Calif.: Communication Research Machines, 1972.

Quirk, John M. "Finding Meaning Every Day." *The International Forum for Logotherapy* 2 (1979), pp. 15–22.

Raskin, David E., and Klein, Zanvel E. "Losing a Symptom Through Keeping It: A Review of Paradoxical Treatment Techniques and Rationale." *Archives of General Psychiatry* 33 (1976): 548–555.

Schachter, Stanley J. "Bettelheim and Frankl: Contradicting Views of the Holocaust." *Reconstructionist* 26 (1961): 6–11.

Solyom L.; Garza-Perez, J.; Ledwidge, B. L.; and Solyom, C. "Paradoxical Intention in the Treatment of Obsessive Thoughts: A Pilot Study." *Comprehensive Psychiatry* 13 (1972): 291–297.

Spiegelberg, Herbert. *Phenomenology in Psychology and Psychiatry.* Evanston, Ill.: Northwestern University Press, 1972.

Takashima, Hiroshi. *Psychosomatic Medicine and Logotherapy.* Foreword by Viktor E. Frankl. Oceanside, N.Y.: Dabor Science Publications, 1977.

Tweedie, Donald F. *Logotherapy and the Christian Faith: An Evaluation of Frankl's Existential Approach to Psychotherapy.* Preface by Viktor E. Frankl. Grand Rapids, Mich.: Baker Book House, 1961.

Ungersma, Aaron J. *The Search for Meaning: A New Approach in Psychotherapy and Pastoral Psychology.* Philadelphia: Westminister Press, 1961. Paperback edition, foreword by Viktor E. Frankl, 1968.

Audiotapes, Videotapes, and Braille Editions

Fabry, Joseph B. *The Pursuit of Meaning: Logotherapy Applied to Life.* Braille edition available on loan at no cost from Woodside Terrace Kiwanis Braille Project, 850 Longview Road, Hillsborough, CA 94010.

Frankl, Viktor E. "Man in Search of Meaning: A Series of Lectures Delivered at the United States International University of San Diego, California." Fourteen ninety-minute cassettes produced by Creative Resources, 4800 West Waco Drive, Waco, TX 76703 ($139.95).

———. *Man's Search for Meaning: An Introduction to Logotherapy.* Braille edition available on loan at no cost from Woodside Terrace Kiwanis Braille Project, 850 Longview Road, Hillsborough, CA 94010.

———. "Man's Search for Meaning: An Introduction to Logotherapy." Recording for the Blind, Inc., 215 East 58th Street, New York, NY 10022.

———. "Meaninglessness: Today's Dilemma." Audiotape produced by Creative Resources, 4800 West Waco Drive, Waco, TX 76703.

———. "Theory and Therapy of Neurosis: A Series of Lectures Delivered at the United States International University in San Diego, California." Eight ninety-minute cassettes produced by Creative Resources, 4800 West Waco Drive, Waco, TX 76703 ($79.95).

———. "Therapy Through Meaning." Psychotherapy Tape Library (P 656), 59 Fourth Avenue, New York, NY 10003 ($10.00).

———. "The Unheard Cry for Meaning:" Audiocassette produced by the Youth Corps, 56 Bond Street, Toronto, Ontario M5B 1X2, Canada ($6.50).

———. "The Unheard Cry for Meaning." Videotape produced by the Youth Corps and Metropolitan Separate School Board of Toronto. Contact Youth Corps, 56 Bond Street, Toronto, Ontario M5B 1X2, Canada (rental fee $10.00).

———. *The Unheard Cry for Meaning: Psychotherapy and Humanism.* Braille edition available on loan at no cost from Woodside Terrace Kiwanis Braille Project, 850 Longview Road, Hillsborough, CA 94010.

———. "Youth in Search of Meaning." Word Cassette Library, 4800 West Waco Drive, Waco, TX 76703 ($4.98).

———. "Youth in Search of Meaning." Audiotape produced by the Youth Corps, 56 Bond Street, Toronto, Ontario M5B 1X2, Canada. Available on reel-to-reel or cassette ($7.50).

———. "Youth in Search of Meaning." Videotape produced by the Youth Corps and Metro Cable Television. Contact Youth Corps, 56 Bond Street, Toronto, Ontario M5B 1X2, Canada (rental fee $10.00).

Gale, Raymond F.; Fabry, Joseph; Finch, Mary Ann; and Leslie, Robert C. "A Conversation with Viktor E. Frankl on Occasion of the Inauguration of the Frankl Library and Memorabilia at the Graduate Theological Union on February 12, 1977," a videotape. Copies may be obtained from Professor Robert C. Leslie, 1798 Scenic Avenue, Berkeley, CA 94709.

Index